Baltimore County:

Celebrating a Legacy

1659 - 2009

350 YEARS
BALTIMORE COUNTY
MARYLAND
1659 - 2009

Dr. Barry A. Lanman

The Historical Society of Baltimore County and the 350th Anniversary Committee gratefully acknowledge and publicly thank the following organizations for their financial support of this publication.

The Baltimore County Commission on Arts and Sciences

The Baltimore County Office of Community Conservation

The Historical Society of Baltimore County

Legacy Web, Baltimore County Public Library

The Maryland Geographic Alliance

The Martha Ross Center for Oral History, Department of History, UMBC

Copyright © 2009 by the Baltimore County Historical Society, Inc.

Baltimore County: Celebrating a Legacy 1659-2009
By: Barry A. Lanman

Published by: The Historical Society of Baltimore County
9811 Van Buren Lane
Cockeysville, MD 21030

Edited by: Jennifer Braithwait Darrow

Design, Layout & Graphics by: Linda A. Schisler

Printed by: United Book Press, Inc.
1807 Whitehead Road
Baltimore, Maryland 21207

Library of Congress Cataloging-in-Publication Data

Lanman, Barry A.
Baltimore County: Celebrating a Legacy 1659-2009 - Barry A. Lanman

ISBN: 978-1-60743-522-8 (hard cover)

ISBN: 978-1-60743-523-5 (soft cover)

Library of Congress Control Number: 2009924402

Edited by

Jennifer Braithwait Darrow

Design, Layout and Graphics

Linda A. Schisler

350th Anniversary Committee

Barbara Yingling, Chair
Phyllis Bailey   William Barry   Ann Blouse   Kevin Clement
Dr. Evart Cornell   Louis S. Diggs   Jason Domasky   Tim Dugan
Dr. Glenn Johnston   Ann E. Kolakowski   Dr. Barry A. Lanman   Tina Nelson
Rex Shepard   Johanna Seymour   Adam Youssi

Coordinator of Research

Johanna Seymour

Research Consultants

John McGrain   Louis S. Diggs   Jason Domasky
Richard Parsons   William Barry

Research, Photographic and Technical Assistance:

Phyllis Bailey   Katie Duncan   Charla Helmers   E. C. Echols
Kevin Webb   John D. Willard V

350th Anniversary Logo

Kerry Skarda and B. Creative Group

Dedications

Baltimore County: Celebrating a Legacy 1659 - 2009 is dedicated to:

The founders of Baltimore County
The residents of Baltimore County, past and present
The families who have made Baltimore County their home for generations
The citizens, who have enabled Baltimore County to grow, prosper and establish a legacy.

Contents

Foreword

Three hundred and fifty years ago, the place we know today as Baltimore County was only a vast, largely unexplored wilderness, at the northern reaches of the Chesapeake Bay. Used seasonally as the hunting grounds of the Susquehanna Indians whose principal home was located further north on the Susquehanna River, the rugged terrain would challenge its first settlers. It would also offer them a future of unlimited potential.

Today's Baltimore County has changed since those early days, but it has always remained a place of boundless opportunity.

For three-and-a-half centuries, generations of families settled here and built some of the strongest, most enduring communities in America. Their struggles and their triumphs helped define the values, traditions and history of our nation. From the earliest days of our colonization to the defense of our liberty at North Point to the construction of an arsenal of democracy at the Glenn L. Martin Aviation Plant in Middle River, the people of Baltimore County helped to forge the character of America.

Neighbors caring about neighbors, understanding that our communities are only as strong as the least of us, and knowing that we are all part of something much greater than ourselves -- these are the values that keep people here and inspire our children to raise their own families in the communities where they themselves grew up.

As you read this book, you will learn about the people, places and events that have made Baltimore County what it is today. Dr. Barry Lanman and his outstanding research teams at the Historical Society of Baltimore County and the University of Maryland, Baltimore County have combined their scholarship and their dedication in order to preserve local history and produce this ceremonial publication in time for the 350th Anniversary of Baltimore County. On behalf of all the people of Baltimore County, I thank them for their efforts.

It is no small accomplishment for a community to prosper for 350 years, and all of us who care about the future of Baltimore County can learn important lessons from the stories of our proud past. Baltimore County is a remarkable community, and as you read our history in this fascinating volume, I know that you will gain an understanding of just how extraordinary we really are.

Baltimore County Executive
Jim Smith

Preface

As a life-long resident of Baltimore County, as well as an educator and author, I was honored when asked to write a publication commemorating the 350th Anniversary of Baltimore County. When the euphoria abated, however, I quickly recognized the responsibility inherent in such an endeavor. I also realized that no one person could adequately produce a volume covering such a diverse set of topics spanning the history of three-and-a-half centuries.

Accordingly, one of my first actions was to assemble a cadre of experts well versed in the history of Baltimore County. Professional historians, citizen historians, students and community organizations enthusiastically responded and came together to assist with the research and the production of an anniversary publication.

Once our vision for the book became clear, the tasks of historical research and resource acquisition began. Settling into a routine, the exploration proceeded in a predictable set of patterns, and by the spring of 2008 I had spent a considerable amount of time in local archives and libraries. The process had become rather mundane, however, that was about to change.

While sitting in the Historical Society of Baltimore County, reviewing several boxes of photographs, my mind started to wander. Suddenly, and without warning, I was transported back to my elementary school classroom in Halethorpe. It was a profound flashback. I could hear my teacher and principal, Miss Emily Jane Brandenburg, talking about local history. Then, I made the connection; it was the spring of 1959 and Miss Brandenburg was telling us that Baltimore County was 300 years old. She shared her favorite stories about the first railroad in the United States running through our community, the Baltimore Aero Meet of 1910 and the Fair of the Iron Horse in 1927. Miss Brandenburg told stories about founders of the community, the development of the neighborhoods and the local citizens who had made the ultimate sacrifice for their homeland during World War I, World War II and Korea. All were stories involving people and events for which she had a great deal of personal knowledge.

In addition to the stories, assigned books and written work, Miss Brandenburg taught us to build displays and dioramas about Baltimore County events and landmarks. She also took us on fieldtrips to places such as the Hampton Mansion.

My mind eventually refocused on the present and I found myself an adult once again in the library surrounded by historical photographs and documents. I realized Miss Brandenburg had given me an amazing gift; one whose significance would take fifty years for me to appreciate. She gave me my first real taste of history as I became intrigued with the stories of fact, lore and legend. While I am sure the nuances of the content were lost on a young boy, I know that the essence of her teaching and her enthusiasm had a profound impact. From this foundation, I developed an interest in history that turned into a career, an avocation and a passion.

To honor Miss Brandenburg and all the individuals who have cultivated the love of Baltimore County history and the joy of learning, my colleagues and I have produced this publication in order to celebrate the 350 year legacy of Baltimore County.

Introduction

Baltimore County, named for Cecilius Calvert the second Lord Baltimore and proprietor of Maryland, is situated in the geographic center of Maryland. Within the confines of its 612 square miles, the third largest political subdivision in the state contains more than twenty-nine identifiable, unincorporated communities. According to recent statistical data, it is the third most populated county in Maryland, with 754,292 inhabitants. Towson, the unincorporated County Seat, holds the distinction of being the largest of its kind in the United States.

Founded in 1659, Baltimore County has been a dynamic political, economic and social force within Maryland throughout its prestigious history. From a national perspective, few local jurisdictions are older than Baltimore County. This fact can be put in context when compared to the founding of Jamestown, Virginia, which recently celebrated its 400th anniversary in 2007. Thus, when some local municipalities around the United States celebrate centennials or even bi-centennials, they are often astonished to learn that Baltimore County is marking an anniversary which spans three-and-a-half centuries.

To commemorate this auspicious occasion, a publication was authorized by the Historical Society of Baltimore County. Funding was obtained through the Baltimore County Commission on Arts and Sciences and the Baltimore County Office of Community Conservation. The conundrum was to produce a ceremonial publication that would effectively celebrate the history of Baltimore County in a single volume and not replicate the works of John McGrain, Richard Parsons, Neal A. Brooks, Eric G Rockel, William C. Hughes, Louis S. Diggs and other local authors. The decision was made to create a publication containing visual images, maps, historical content and the personal memories of Baltimore Countians arranged in thematic chapters by chronology. To augment the inclusion of the people, places and events that are representative of the County's history throughout its distinct geographic regions, overarching strands relating to the concepts of tradition, change and diversity are presented as an additional interpretive element.

In order to accomplish the goals and parameters set forth for this book, more than 4,000 images were reviewed, of which approximately 450 were selected to represent this complex and extensive heritage. Throughout the chapters, images were identified from many of the classic photographs previously published over time in a variety of sources. An extensive effort was made to acquire unpublished photographs which represent a "new" interpretation of life in Baltimore County. Some photographs were collected from archives, but many others came from attics, shoeboxes and personal scrapbooks. Accordingly, the reminiscences of a collective heritage were obtained from prominent citizens as well as from those individuals who live in relative obscurity yet provide the essence of everyday life within this local region. The words and images gathered from all strata of existence paint a realistic and representative portrait of Baltimore County past and present; a view that can be perused by future readers as an anniversary "time capsule."

The 350th Anniversary Committee expects that readers will obtain an appreciation of Baltimore County's past as chronicled in terms of its historical events which illuminate the natural resources, distinct places, architectural structures, various modes of transportation, inventors, entrepreneurs, military leaders, politicians and visionaries. In addition, it is hoped that the publication conveys the true heritage of the County; the generations of everyday citizens with diverse backgrounds who labored to make a living, raise a family and at the same time turn a wilderness into a thriving municipality. It is to this spirit of achievement that Baltimore County owes a debt of gratitude, for it is this mosaic of individuals who created a legacy upon which today's citizens of Baltimore County can build their future.

Chapter 1

ESTABLISHING A LEGACY

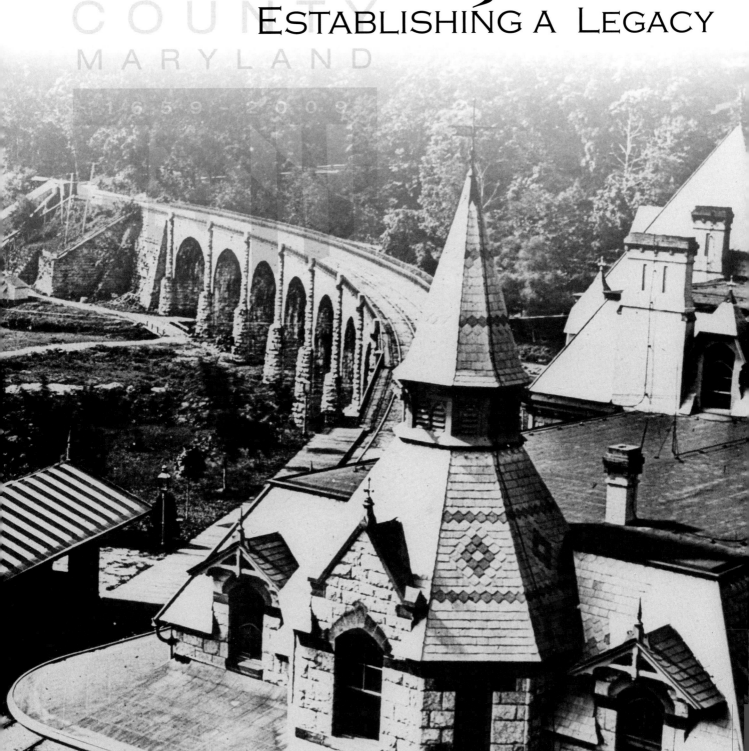

In 1634, George and Leonard Calvert set foot on the shores of Maryland at St. Clements Island along with 104 settlers. Shortly thereafter, adventurers, explorers and others in search of opportunity made their way to the land which would later be known as Baltimore County. While speculation suggests that the municipality may have been created through a proclamation issued by the Governor of Maryland, no actual record of this decree survives. In the absence of such documentation, the first definitive reference to the municipality was recorded on January 12, 1659 when an order was issued to the County Sheriff requesting that he arrange an election of burgesses to represent Baltimore County in the next session of the General Assembly. However, it would be another fifteen years before formal boundaries were delineated and other governmental functions put into action. From this meager beginning, a dynamic region emerged.

During the County's earliest days, subsistence agriculture was imperative to the survival of the small band of settlers. However, as time progressed, land patents were granted, the population increased and an economic system slowly took shape which contributed to the overall productivity of the region. Firmly established during the eighteenth century and continuing into the nineteenth century, the economy expanded beyond its agricultural base to include limekilns, mining, ironworks and a variety of mills. With an abundance of natural resources, strategic proximity to water, and the addition of roads and railways, the municipality continued to expand.

In addition to the aforementioned aspects of its past, Baltimore County's military history, lore and legend serve as proud reminders of its legacy. From the Revolutionary War and the War of 1812 to the Civil War, Baltimore County has been defined by its prowess in defense of its shores and protection of its citizens before the dawn of the twentieth century.

Thus, in order to adequately represent Baltimore County's extensive history during its formative years, Establishing a Legacy is a unique chapter in this publication. Rather than concentrating on a specific theme and tracing it through to the current day, this chapter provides an overview of the initial elements of Baltimore County history. Eighteenth and ninetieth century transportation, industry, houses and mansions are depicted through paintings, drawings and the earliest photographs known to exist. In the same manner, the human element is visually represented, including men and women who established towns, founded industries, developed organizations, formed institutions, produced inventions and served in the military. Therefore, the chapter chronicles a history of the people, places and events, which acting in confluence, established the foundation of a legacy and created a place as unique as Baltimore County.

"History is who we are and why we are the way we are."

David C. McCullough

Upon acquiring the colonial charter for Maryland, so named for Queen Henrietta Marie, the wife of the King, Cecil the Second Lord Baltimore sent his two brothers, George and Leonard Calvert to lead an expedition. The Ark and the Dove brought them, along with 140 colonists, to the shores of Maryland in March, 1634. Colonization of Maryland soon followed. (Artwork courtesy of the Enoch Pratt Free Library)

Once in the Colony of Maryland, George Calvert and his brother granted land patents along the bay to prominent settlers. Twenty-five years later, Baltimore County came into existence because of the availability of natural resources and reasonable access to water. (Painting courtesy of the Enoch Pratt Free Library)

CHARLES CARROLL OF CARROLLTON.

Charles Carroll of Carrollton, who was among the signers of the Declaration of Independence, was a major land owner and an investor in Baltimore County enterprise. Carroll along with his partners, the Ellicott Brothers, convinced farmers to grow wheat rather than tobacco, thus providing the natural resources for their gristmills. Outliving Adams, Jefferson and all the other signers of the Declaration of Independence, Carroll was an investor in the Baltimore & Ohio Railroad before his death at the age of ninety-five. (Painting courtesy of the Catonsville Room, Baltimore County Public Library)

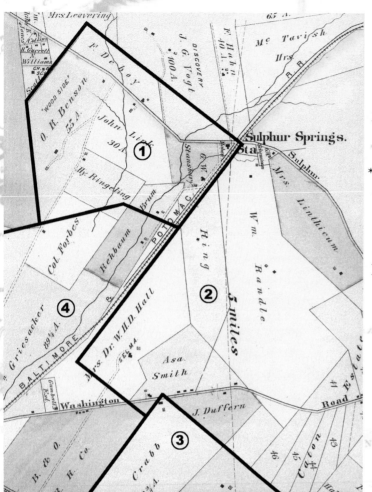

Colonial land patents granted in the northern part of a Baltimore County were generally larger than the patents in the southwest area of the county. The examples of patents researched by George Horvath: 1. "Ropers Increase" 1668 2. "Yates Forbearance" 1683 3. "Yates Enlarged" circa 1680 4. "United Friendship" 1687. These patents ranged in size from 770 acres to 1800 acres. *Note: The 1877 map of southwestern Baltimore County, created by G.M. Hopkins, was used as a geographical reference point and the patents were overlaid on the Hopkins' Map. The four patents covered current sections of Arbutus, Halethorpe and Lansdowne. (Map courtesy of George Horvath)

Fort Garrison, built circa 1693 and believed to be the oldest surviving structure in Baltimore County, served for a few years as the headquarters for a troop of mounted rangers who guarded against potentially hostile Native Americans. Never having experienced any hostilities, the Fort was enlarged to two stories and served as a farm building which housed slaves in the eighteenth and nineteenth centuries. The structure has been preserved and externally restored by Baltimore County, its frontier origins mark a striking contrast amidst the surrounding development. (Photograph courtesy of the Baltimore County Public Library)

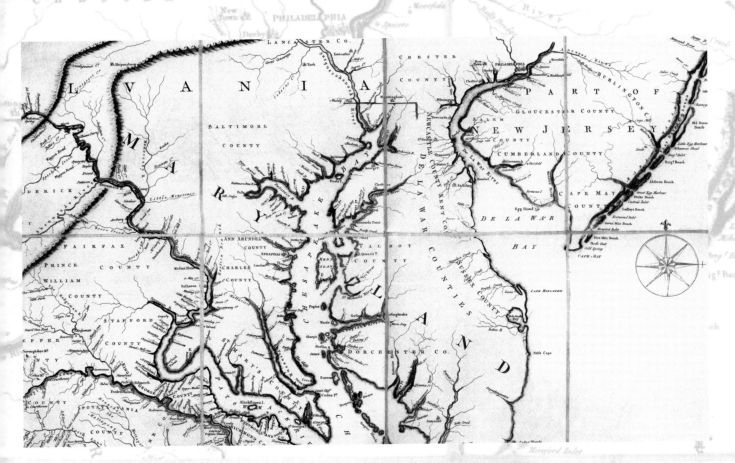

Originally, Baltimore County's boundary lines were not well defined. In fact, they were more of an approximation of territory and included present day Baltimore City, Cecil, Kent, Harford and parts of Anne Arundel, Carroll and Howard counties. This 1735 map shows the size of Baltimore County in the early part of the eighteenth century. From that time, as other counties were formed, Baltimore County was diminished but its present borders were not finalized until 1918. (Map courtesy of the Maryland Historical Society)

Benjamin Banneker was born on November 9, 1731 near an area that would become Ellicott's Mills. As a free man, he was mostly self-educated and served as a technical assistant in the calculating and first-ever surveying of what would become the District of Columbia. He also developed an expertise in astronomy and was the first African American scientist. Banneker was a champion for the abolition of slavery and civil rights until his death in 1806. A park commemorating Benjamin Banneker is located at the former site of Banneker's farm in the Oella area of Baltimore County. (Graphic courtesy of the Catonsville Room, Baltimore County Public Library)

In the eighteenth century, a branch of the Worthington family developed their holdings into a huge plantation extending from Old Court Road south and west almost to the Patapsco River. Their slaves and the slaves of other property owners in the area used to roll hogsheads of tobacco and dry goods to Rag Landing, the landing on the Baltimore County bank. Thus, the road became known as Rolling Road. While this heritage is generally well known, it is not widely known that Baltimore County actually had several "rolling roads" for generally the same purpose.

(Drawing courtesy of the Catonsville Room, Baltimore County Public Library)

Richard Caton, was an entrepreneur like his father-in-law, Charles Carroll of Carrollton; however, he was not as astute a business man. While in financial distress, Carroll carefully partnered with Caton in the ownership of land in the southwest section of Baltimore County. Over time, the disposal of the land and the Frederick Turnpike contributed to the development of Catonsville. (Painting courtesy of the Catonsville Room, Baltimore County Public Library)

Fort Howard, North Point, has many distinctive historic stories. In 1790, it was the landing location for the ferry that crossed the Chesapeake Bay from Kent Island, connecting with stagecoaches for the bumpy ride along North Point Road (Old Log Lane) to Baltimore. Most scholars believe that the invading British troops, on the morning of September 12, 1814, landed along the shoreline immediately north of the present Fort property. It was realized, before the Spanish-American War, that Baltimore Harbor was defenseless against an enemy naval fleet such as Spain. Thus, the remaining fortifications were begun in 1896. After the Fort was decommissioned in 1940, the property became a Veterans Administration Hospital and County Park. (Photograph courtesy of John McGrain and the Historical Society of Baltimore County)

Charles Ridgley (1733-1790) was the builder of Hampton Mansion. Along with being a plantation owner, he was a sea captain, merchant and iron master. This portrait was painted by John Hesselius. (Painting courtesy of the Hampton National Historic Site, National Park Service)

Rebecca Dorsey Ridgley (1739-1812) was the wife of Charles Ridgley. Rebecca moved to the Auburn House after her husband's death. The Auburn House is currently located on the campus of Towson University, however, most of the original house had to be rebuilt after a major fire. (Painting courtesy of the Hampton National Historic Site, National Park Service)

A recent photograph of the Hampton Mansion shows the north facade of the Georgian manor house built between 1783 and 1790 by more than ninety slaves. The structure, known as the "Hampton House" was one of the largest privately owned residences in America at that time. While the Ridgleys amassed thousands of acres of property, most of the land was sold in the nineteenth and twentieth centuries. However, the mansion and several acres of land stayed in the Ridgley Family until 1948. It is now a museum run by the National Park Service. (Photograph courtesy of the Hampton National Historic Site, National Park Service)

The terraced formal gardens south of the mansion were well manicured, circa 1878. Two hundred and fifty additional flower beds existed on the property. Hampton also had the largest citrus tree collection in the United States during the mid-nineteenth century. (Photograph courtesy of the Hampton National Historic Site, National Park Service)

While the Northampton Furnace started to produce pig iron in 1761, it was not until the Revolutionary War that the business became highly successful due to the increased demand for iron products. Thus, the furnace produced cannon, shot, guns and camp kettles during the war. This fireback was also cast at the furnace, circa 1775. Farming and stone quarrying also produced a large part of the Ridgley fortune. (Photograph courtesy of the Hampton National Historic Site, National Park Service)

Nancy Davis was one of a large contingent of slaves who labored at Hampton. Freed before the Civil War, she continued to work for the Ridgley family until her death in 1908 and was buried in the Ridgley Family cemetery. Eliza Ridgley (1858-1954) was photographed with Nancy. (Photograph courtesy of the Hampton National Historic Site, National Park Service)

Patapsco Mill A, one of three mills owned by the Charles A. Gambrill Manufacturing Company, came into existence, circa 1772 and was located in Ellicott City, once a part of Baltimore County. Capable of producing 200 barrels of flour a day, it was the largest mill of its type in colonial America. Their flour, known as the Patapsco Brand, was the first American flour to seek a general market. (Drawing courtesy of the Catonsville Room, Baltimore County Public Library)

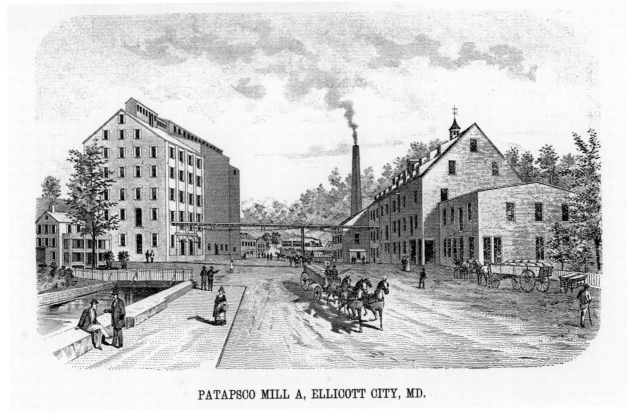

PATAPSCO MILL A, ELLICOTT CITY, MD.

Ballestone/Stansbury Manor, a Federal-style mansion located in Essex, is a beautiful example of a middle class home of the era. While a great deal of the structure's history has yet to be fully documented, the mansion was purchased in 1969 by Baltimore County and placed on the National Register of Historic Places in 1975. The property was restored as a nonprofit living-history museum and exhibit space. (Photograph courtesy of Jonathan M. Cornell)

Shaw's Discovery, located on Bauers Farm Lane near Edgemere, was built in two integrated parts, in 1783 and 1794, for the Shaw family. It served as a mid-sized plantation of that era. Despite its shabby appearance in the photo, which is to be corrected by restoration, this is the only remaining structure on Patapsco Neck that witnessed the advance of the invading British troops in September 1814 and their withdrawal two days later after the Battle of Baltimore. (Photograph courtesy of John McGrain and the Historical Society of Baltimore County)

An engraving of an incident in the War of 1812 rendered a patriotic version of Nathan Towson, on foot with sword, ready to take action against British gun positions under the direction of General Winfield Scott on horseback. Nathan Towson was a Captain at the time but later rose to the ranks of Paymaster General of the U.S. Army. (Engraving courtesy of the Baltimore County Public Library)

The Battle of North Point took place against the British during the defense of Baltimore in the War of 1812. This engraving was designed, painted and published by Thomas Ruckle, an amateur artist from Baltimore. The scene, painted in 1831, depicted the Battle on September 12, 1814. While a tactical loss for Brigadier General John Stricker and his men, the Battle of North Point proved to be a strategic victory for the overall defense of Baltimore. (Engraving courtesy of the Maryland Historical Society and the Baltimore County Public Library)

During the War of 1812, several men are known for their exploits and heroism. Among them are General Robert Ross, who was mortally wounded at the Battle of North Point, Major General Samuel Smith and Francis Scott Key. However, Joshua Barney is an unknown hero. After serving in the Continental Navy during the American Revolution, Barney joined the U.S. Navy and commanded the Chesapeake Bay Flotilla, a fleet of gunboats defending the bay. His use of shallow barges with large guns worked perfectly against the British and allowed for retreat in the shallow waters of the Chesapeake for safety. Commodore Barney, who was born and lived in Baltimore, died in 1818 from complications related to the wound he received at the Battle of Bladensburg. Several U.S. Navy ships have been named in his honor. (Painting courtesy of the Maryland Historical Society)

The production of lime was a major industry in Baltimore County during the eighteenth and nineteenth centuries. Limekilns were used until World War I for burning limestone to produce lime for de-acidifying agricultural land. Lime was also used in the production of white wash. The Krause Memorial Lime Kiln, located on Old Harford Road in Carney is a restored example of a nineteenth century kiln. It is now the

centerpiece of a neighborhood County park. (Photograph courtesy of John McGrain and the Historical Society of Baltimore

Textile, flour and gristmill production accounted for the bulk of the Baltimore County economy before the Civil War. Rockland Mill was first established as a flour mill on Falls Road at Old Court Road in 1813, however, by 1855, it had become a cotton factory. This photograph of the mill was taken in 1905. (Photograph courtesy of the Baltimore County Public Library)

One of the oldest mills in Baltimore County was Milford Mill, established in 1728 by Richard Gist. However, Mitchell Mill, also called Summerfield Mill, was the most photographed of all the mills in the county due to its "classic" look. The mill was located on Cub Hill Road and remained in operation until it burned in 1903. The gristmill could produce, like most of its competitors, 200-300 barrels of flour a day during the mid-nineteenth century. (Photograph courtesy of the Baltimore County Public Library)

In the 1820s, Baltimore was the third largest city in the United States and was in competition with New York and Philadelphia for the domination of western trade. Thus, a group of businessmen received a charter on February 28, 1827 to build the Baltimore and Ohio Railroad. The first section of the B&O was completed between Baltimore City and Ellicott's Mills by May of 1830. The first railroad cars looked like stage coaches, drawn by horses over straps of iron mounted on wood which rested on ties. By October 1, 1831, 81,905 people had paid 75 cents to ride this new technological marvel. (Graphic courtesy of the Catonsville Room, Baltimore County Public Library)

This drawing of Pikesville Arsenal may have been rendered by Baltimore artist Frank Blackwell Mayer. The rendering was completed in 1845. While peaceful at the time, fifteen years later, the arsenal would be well fortified at the beginning of the Civil War. (Drawing courtesy of the Baltimore County Public Library)

13

In 1844, Professor Samuel F. B. Morse created the first working electromagnetic telegraph system which ran between Baltimore and Washington D.C. The formal dispatch "WHAT HATH GOD WROUGHT?" was the first telegraph message sent and it traveled through Baltimore County on May 24, 1844. By the Civil War, the telegraph had changed the expectations for the speed with which communications took place. (Photograph courtesy of Special Collections, Albin O. Kuhn Library and Gallery, University of Maryland, Baltimore County)

George Kephart was the owner of Walnut Grove Farm. In 1879, he donated land so that the All Saints Episcopal Church could be built along with a cemetery. Kephart also gave permission to the local African American community to erect a church on land he had given them after the Civil War. St. Luke's Church still stands on Bond Avenue. (Photograph courtesy of the Baltimore County Public Library)

In 1886, the Jones family held a centennial celebration at their ancestral home in Walnut Grove. The property was originally granted to the Jones family from the Lords Baltimore. The highlights of the day were the group photograph and a balloon ascension. Thus, the celebration of heritage has been a long-standing tradition in Baltimore County. (Photograph courtesy of Heritage Society of Essex and Middle River)

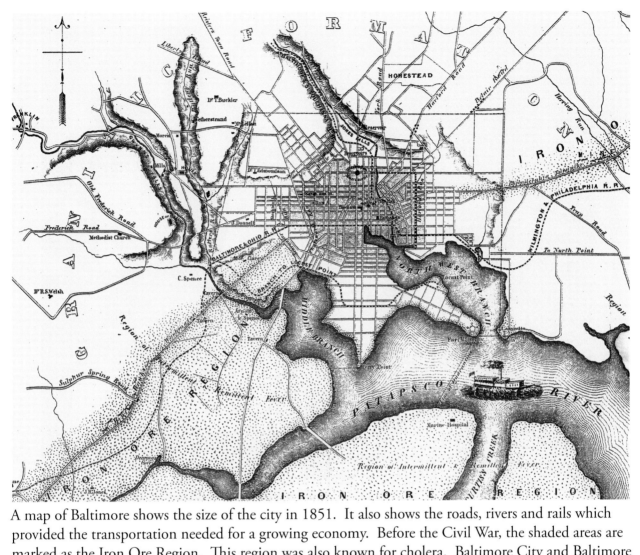

A map of Baltimore shows the size of the city in 1851. It also shows the roads, rivers and rails which provided the transportation needed for a growing economy. Before the Civil War, the shaded areas are marked as the Iron Ore Region. This region was also known for cholera. Baltimore City and Baltimore County would officially separate in 1854. (Map courtesy of the Historical Society of Baltimore County)

The Running Pump Tavern, circa the 1890s, was a center of commerce on Reisterstown and Village Roads in Pikesville. Horse and mule drawn covered wagons were still being used to traverse many of the yet unpaved roads. (Photograph courtesy of the Baltimore County Public Library)

Benjamin Henry Latrobe, II, son of the architect who designed the United States Capitol, was chosen to design the railroad bridge that would connect Baltimore with Washington D.C. Named for the founder and the first president of the B&O Railroad, Phillip E. Thomas, the bridge became known as the Thomas Viaduct. Stretching 612 feet and standing 60 feet high the bridge contained eight arches. The structure also had the distinction of being the first stone, arched, bridge built on a curved alignment. The Thomas Viaduct opened on July 4, 1835. Because of its logistics, the bridge was considered to be one of the most strategic sites of the Civil War. (Photograph courtesy of the Catonsville Room, Baltimore County Public Library)

The original entrance to Loudon Park Cemetery was designed by architect S. Sloan in the 1850s. The cemetery was part of Baltimore County until the boundary lines changed and it became part of Baltimore City. The horse-drawn trolley car of the Baltimore, Catonsville and Ellicott's Mills Passenger Railway operated from 1860 to 1898, after which it was electrified and run as part of a system which lasted until the 1960s. (Photograph courtesy of the Baltimore County Public Library)

The combined portraits represent many prominent landowners, business men, military men and educators, circa the 1870s. Among the leaders of Baltimore were Colonel William Allen, Headmaster of McDonogh; Lloyd Howard of Grey Rock and Pikesville; John McHenry of Sudbrook; Dr. William Wood, Rosewood; Dr. John Fisher, founder of Goucher College; and George Elder of Green Spring. (Photograph courtesy of the Baltimore County Public Library)

The original Pikesville Arsenal was used as the Confederate Soldiers Home on Reisterstown Road in Pikesville. Confederate veterans were photographed on the benches in front of the Arsenal in 1911. The property became the State Police Training Academy in the 1950s and later served as the Headquarters of the Maryland State Police. The Boy Scouts also used the building as a meeting site in the 1940s. (Photograph courtesy of the Baltimore County Public Library)

Gilmor's Raid and the cavalry movement of General Bradley T. Johnson were the only significant Confederate actions that took place in Baltimore County during the Civil War. Thus, the County was spared major battles. However, Baltimore, like Maryland, had split allegiance during the Civil War. Thus, separate facilities were necessary for the care of Union and Confederate veterans after the war. Maryland Line Confederate Soldiers were housed at the Confederate Soldiers Home from 1888 to 1932. (Photograph courtesy of the Catonsville Room, Baltimore County Public Library)

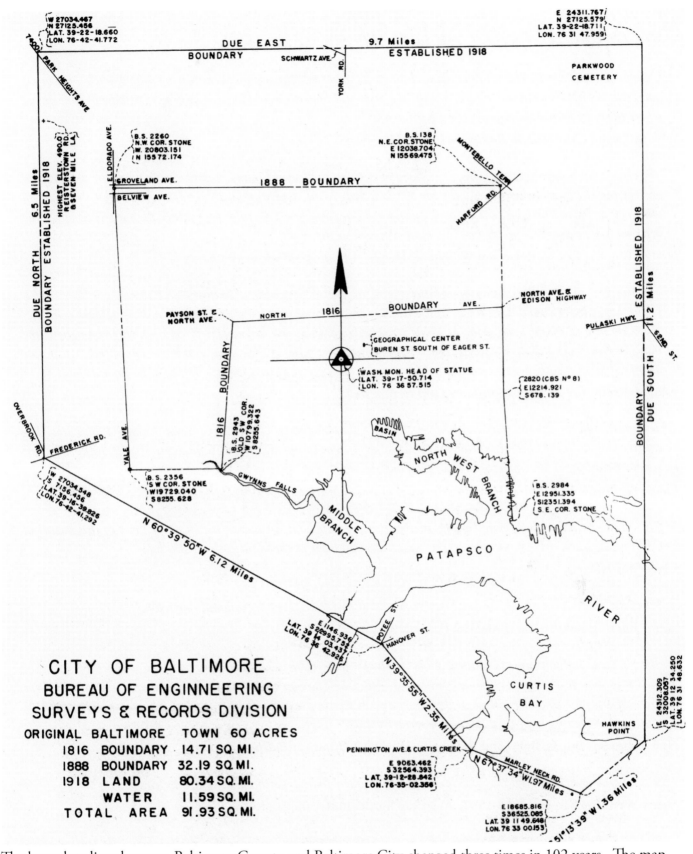

The boundary lines between Baltimore County and Baltimore City changed three times in 102 years. The map shows the size of the city in 1816, 1888 and 1918. Since they saw themselves as radically different jurisdictions, economic, political and philosophical conflicts occurred. The County and the City formally separated in 1854. (Map courtesy of Baltimore City, Division of Surveys and Records)

Baltimore County Memories . . .

"Unless one visits a mill and vibrates along with its laboring machinery and breathes the dust particles, history is only so many lifeless words on a page. Unlike the history of bloodshed and battles, milling is a phase of Americana where the onlooker would enjoy being a participant."

- **John McGrain,** *Grist Mills in Baltimore County, Maryland*

"The occasional bumpy road or infrequent potholes that are the bane of many motorists' existence were an accepted part of travel in earlier centuries…during the last century all roads constantly needed repairs and were strewn with ruts or holes. Travel seemed more often an adventure and a test of endurance rather than a means of getting between two points. Few people had any kind remarks for the roads."

- **Neal A. Brooks, Eric G. Rokel and William C. Hughs,** *A History of Baltimore County*

"The Ridgelys made a fortune by combining their pursuits of agriculture, industry and commerce. This success allowed the family to maintain a way of life realized by few Americans in the eighteenth and nineteenth centuries. Their lavish and comfortable mode of living was made possible by a large work force, operating throughout the many outbuildings and dependencies. Only by relating the activities of these areas and the servants and craftspeople who facilitated the life of ease within the Mansion can we hope to gain a realistic image of Hampton's past."

- **John McGrain,** *Grist Mills in Baltimore County, Maryland*

"The courthouse in Towson was designed in 1854 by Thomas Dixon, James Dixon and Thomas Balbirnie. The courthouse was built of local marble and limestone. It was completed in 1856 at a cost of $30,000…The first indoor plumbing in Towson was in the courthouse."

- **Elaine Bunting and Patricia D'Amario,** *Counties of North Maryland*

"My ancestors came to Baltimore County in 1790. All generations, including myself, have lived in this beautiful County ever since. My grandfather, father and I were all born in the house where I still live."

- **Clyde Morris, Freeland**

"Pikesville was named after Zebulon Pike…who discovered Pike's Peak in Colorado in 1806."

- **Elaine Bunting and Patricia D'Amario,** *Counties of North Maryland*

"The Shawnee Indians came to Baltimore County in the late 1670s, and they apparently used this area as a temporary home until the 1710s. The Shawan area in central Baltimore County may have been the site of a Shawnee village at this time, and at least one authority believes that Johnny Cake Road in the southwestern county is a corruption of the term, 'Shawnee Cake'."

- **Neal A. Brooks, Eric G. Rokel and William C. Hughs,** *A History of Baltimore County*

"It is truly said of Hampton that it expresses more grandeur than any other place in America."

- **Henry Winthrop Sargent, 1810-1882, American horticulturist and landscape gardener**

"The men and women of early Baltimore County were hard working, energetic and materialistic. The nature of the colonial experience required such a life style…The games of early settlers reflected their lifestyle, with cock fighting, eye gouging and wrestling the most popular. This was not an easy life, but a life of simple self-sufficiency."

- **Neal A. Brooks, Eric G. Rokel and William C. Hughs,** *A History of Baltimore County*

"Dundalk Armory is host to the 175th Infantry, which stopped the British from marching on Baltimore in 1814. The 175th Infantry recently returned from serving in Iraq."

- **Joseph Gutierrez, Maryland National Guard**

"I love living in Baltimore County because of all the history that happened here, like the Battle of North Point."

- **Honor Bowerman, Age 10, Lutherville**

"The horse has been a vital element in the history of Baltimore County…Early English immigrants brought the tradition of fox hunting to Baltimore County, which eventually led to the first recognized steeplechase race run on October 18, 1873, north of Pimlico in Baltimore County. The first Maryland Hunt Cup was run in 1894. Polo, jousting, fox hunting and equestrian teams blossomed in the area."

- **Janey Mowell, Glencoe**

"Mitchell's Mill is an old picturesque mill, surrounded by towering hills, with a fussy little brook tumbling over rocks in front of it, on its way to the Gunpowder."

- ***Baltimore County Union,*** **1893**

"Some interesting names for towns in Baltimore County include Boring, Sweet Air, Sparks, Maryland Line, Sunnybrook, Shane, Butler, Delight, Chase and Texas."

- **Elaine Bunting and Patricia D'Amario, *Counties of North Maryland***

"Noted for its scenic beauty, Baltimore County has, since colonial times, been the seat of magnificent and historic residences…Many noted statesmen and military leaders have called it their home."

- **J. Millard Tawes, Governor of Maryland, 1959-1967**

"It's a rare thing that several generations of my family have been able to share the same schools, roads, homes and businesses."

- **Jayme Schomann, Timonium**

"I am proud of my Baltimore County heritage. Over 124 years ago, my great-great-grandfather, Henry Gunther, and great-grandfather Peter Schultz, purchased and farmed land in North Point, now called Fort Howard. The Gunther and Schultz families still live in the County."

- **Janet M. Gunther, North Point**

"I'm a lifelong resident of Baltimore County, having been born and raised in Eastwood, one of the communities that makes up the Southeast part of the County. I will forever be a citizen of this great County, which has so much to offer. Farmland, urban areas, terrific communities with individual pride making up the whole mosaic of one of the oldest and best counties in the nation. Representing the 7th District of Baltimore County has been an honor for me. When I think about the history and progress and future plans for Baltimore County it is with the greatest pride. In this 21st century, we can reflect back on our beginnings and see the tremendous growth that has occurred. As we look to the future, I see Baltimore County continuing along its path in being one of the outstanding counties in the country."

- **John Olszewski, Sr., Baltimore County Councilman, 7st District**

350 YEARS
BALTIMORE
COUNTY
MARYLAND
1659 - 2009

Chapter 2

HOMES & ESTATES

*T*he American dream of home ownership has been a motivating factor for settlement in Baltimore County since the first explorers traveled through the environs of the region. Despite the passage of time, successive generations have shared this universal aspiration.

For those who were granted large colonial land patents, like the Ridgleys, Catons and Worthingtons, massive estates were built. In contrast, structures for indentured servants and slaves were usually tiny wooden structures with dirt floors. Most residents, of working class status, built and lived in modest structures with simplistic amenities. Thus, mixed throughout the landscape, houses of varying sizes and styles reflected a stratified society.

A factor which had profound impact on Baltimore County's housing in the nineteenth century was the development of mill towns to accommodate the requisite workforce. Ellicott's Mills, Warren, Ashland and Sparrows Point, among others, became self-sufficient places for people to work and live without the need for transportation. Company housing, both a blessing and a curse, provided protection from the elements and often served as an interim step to home ownership. Many of these towns endured long after the original industry ceased to exist. A similar phenomenon occurred during the industrial booms which occurred as a result of World War I and World War II.

While company housing had a marked influence on the living patterns for a large segment of the population in the County, so did real estate developers who responded to the demand for housing, especially after World War II. Apartment complexes, townhouse communities and entire subdivisions, with quarter-acre lots seemed to appear overnight and had a way of modifying the American Dream for many families.

By comparison with other eras, today's residential choices in Baltimore County seem endless. Restored Victorian homes with wrap-around porches, center hall colonials, bungalows and ranch houses are but a few of the selections available around the County. Multi-density cluster homes, garage town homes, luxury apartments and condominiums are also options available for those with a busy lifestyle. While these types of structures are changing the face of residential Baltimore County, the most dramatic transformation is occurring in Towson as a result of a billion dollar program of residential and commercial development which will ultimately re-configure the skyline and demographics of the County Seat.

Despite the choices and options, locations and expense, one commonality remains: The enduring hope of individuals to own a piece of Baltimore County and to create a place which they can call home.

"Home is a place you grow up wanting to leave, and grow old wanting to get back to."

John Ed Pearce

Taylor's Hall, a telescoping house, was built about 1735 by Joseph Taylor and was acquired in 1791 by Thomas Cockey Daye. It was later owned by the Harry T. Campbell family of quarrying fame. This photograph shows the structure in 1975 before it was moved in 1986 to the Brooklandville area by Martin P. Azola. (Photograph courtesy of the Baltimore County Public Library)

A drawing by Frank B. Mayer shows Howard's Square at Grey Rock as it looked in 1846. The stone house was built in the eighteenth century by Cornelius Howard. His son, John Eager Howard, a Revolutionary War Hero, was born in the house. (Drawing courtesy of the Baltimore County Public Library)

The estate Long Island is located on Cromwell Bridge Road and was built between 1744 and 1830. The property has a rich history relating to agriculture and commerce in the Towson area. Circuit Court Judge, Walter M. Jennifer owned the estate in the 1970s when this photograph was taken. Efforts are under way to preserve this unique structure and grounds. (Photograph courtesy of the Baltimore County Public Library)

This view of Perry Hall Mansion was taken around 1890 when it was owned by William George Dunty. The house was built by Corbin Lee, an ironmaster, who died in 1773 before construction was completed. Like most houses of its era, it was partially consumed by fire, rebuilt and subsequently had several owners. (Photograph courtesy of the Baltimore County Public Library)

While not at its peak, as shown in 1966, Timonium Mansion was located near the northwest corner of York and Timonium Roads. The estate was originally named Belle Field when it was built in the early 1780s by Archibald Buchanan. However, it was renamed Timonium in 1786 by Sarah Lee Buchanan after the death of her husband. The mansion was torn down in 1977 to make way for commercial development. (Photograph courtesy of the Baltimore County Public Library)

The English Consul Mansion, located on Oak Grove Road in English Consul, was built between 1818 and 1830 by William Dawson on a 300 acre estate. Dawson was the first English Consul to Baltimore after the War of 1812. (Photograph courtesy of the Baltimore County Public Library)

This marvelous structure, an eighteenth century bathhouse, is located on the grounds of Trentham in Owings Mills. (Photograph courtesy of the Baltimore County Public Library)

Ice houses were a necessity before refrigeration. This elaborate ice house was located on the corner of York and Shawan Road. It was later rehabilitated by O'Connor, Piper & Flynn Realty in the 1980s and used as a sales outlet. (Photograph courtesy of the Baltimore County Public Library)

In order to cure and preserve meats, smoke houses were typical outbuildings on rural properties in Baltimore County. This brick smoke house at the Everett Partridge House on Hunter Mill Road in White Hall is a remnant of an era gone by. (Photograph courtesy of the Baltimore County Public Library)

The Oliver House, located on Gunpowder Road, was designed by Robert Mills for Robert Oliver, one of Baltimore's first merchant millionaires and co-founder of the Baltimore & Ohio Railroad. This 26-room mansion was built in 1821 and accommodated Oliver and his friends as a hunting and fishing lodge. The enormous estate included a "deer park" with more than 300 domesticated deer. (Photograph courtesy of John McGrain and the Historical Society of Baltimore County)

Ravenshurst, once located on Antique Lane in the Long Green vicinity, was transformed from a modest stone farmhouse into a thirty-eight room hilltop mansion probably before the Civil War. Its most famous owner was Major General I. Ridgeway Trimble. Unfortunately for Ravenshurst, an accident during a restoration project, in 1985, caused the grand building's destruction in a fire as spectacular as its architectural flourishes. (Photograph courtesy of John McGrain and the Historical Society of Baltimore County)

The Alto Dale Estate on Reisterstown Road in Pikesville was owned by Dr. John Goucher, founder of Goucher College. Dr. Goucher entertained "Goucher Girls" with parties on the lawn of his mansion built in 1859. Dr. Goucher died in 1922 and the house was subsequently purchased by Baltimore industrialist Jacob Blaustein. (Photograph courtesy of the Baltimore County Public Library)

Built as a summer cottage in 1889-1890, this house was designated as Cottage #10 in Sudbrook Park. Sudbrook Park was a subdivision built in 1889 on John Howard McHenry's Sudbrook Estate. The 845 acre property was designed by Frederick Law Olmstead. Like Catonsville and many other Baltimore County communities, Sudbrook started out as a summer retreat for affluent residents of Baltimore City. (Photograph courtesy of the Baltimore County Public Library)

Thornton, the Rider-Bushman House, 1812 Landrake Road, Riderwood. Occupied a hilltop overlooking the once bucolic view of Roland Run, Thorton was built before 1877 for the prominent Rider family, and was subsequently enlarged. From 1916 to 1920 it was the home of silent-screen idol Francis X. Bushman, the star of *Ben Hur.* He also starred in at least 179 other silent films. (Photograph courtesy of John McGrain and the Historical Society of Baltimore County)

Located in Eden Terrace, Catonsville, Arden was owned by Victor Bloede and was a grandiose estate before it burned in 1898 as a result of a Christmas Tree Fire. (Photograph courtesy of the Baltimore County Public Library)

This massive mansion on Park Heights Avenue in Stevenson was originally built as a wedding present for Henriette Louise Cromwell in 1917. While a wealthy and prominent family, the mansion's highest profile occupant was General Douglas MacArthur when he became Cromwell's second husband. However, the marriage was short-lived and ended in 1929. After several residential ownerships, the mansion transitioned into the sedate Baptist Home of Maryland. Sold again, circa 2005, the mansion is again a private residence. (Photograph courtesy of John McGrain and the Historical Society of Baltimore County)

As the sign states, lots in Catonsville's Oak Forest Park could be purchased for under $500, circa 1920. While the roads were not yet paved, cement sidewalks were being constructed. Gas, electricity and water were available at this suburban site. (Photograph courtesy of the Catonsville Room, Baltimore County Public Library)

This house on Burke Avenue was a "Sears Catalog" house and was built in 1921. Several homes throughout the Baltimore County area were built from prefabricated kits like this one. (Photograph courtesy of the Baltimore County Public Library)

The Galloway-Dickey House, located on Baltimore National Pike near Catonsville, was built in 1920 for Charles W. Galloway, the Vice President for Operations and Maintenance of the vast Baltimore & Ohio Railroad. Galloway served the B&O Railroad for fifty-seven years but died before he could become President. The house is a handsome example of a Craftsman-style bungalow. (Photograph courtesy of John McGrain and the Historical Society of Baltimore County)

This view of the 200 block of E Street in Sparrows Point shows the typical row houses in the area, circa 1929. They were rented by steel workers and were modest but comfortable examples of company housing during that era. (Photograph courtesy of the Baltimore County Public Library)

Westview Park was a typical housing development built in the 1950s and 1960s. Ranch houses on a quarter-acre lot were in high demand at a price tag under $20,000. This view from the air speaks to the lack of individuality expressed in the design of tract housing; a site replicated by builders during this era of suburban growth. (Photograph courtesy of the Historical Society of Baltimore County)

Hampton Plaza, a fashionable condominium building constructed in 1969, was located on East Joppa Road at the corner of Fairmount Avenue in Towson. The condominium represented the interest in high density housing in various sections of Baltimore County; a trend that continues to the current day. (Photograph courtesy of the Baltimore County Public Library)

For some Baltimore County residents with demanding careers, not having a yard to mow is an advantage. Thus, condominiums have been a popular part of residential revitalization in the center of Towson over the past several years. (Photograph courtesy of the Baltimore County Office of Communications)

While modern housing is often a choice and a necessity at times, many citizens have enjoyed restoring a "classic" home with a front porch. This lovely home is located in Oak Forest, Catonsville and was built about a century ago. (Photograph courtesy of the Baltimore County Office of Communications)

Due to the expense of land and the escalating cost of building supplies, townhouses like condominiums have become an alternative housing option to the single family home. (Photograph courtesy of the Baltimore County Office of Communications)

Baltimore County Memories . . .

"I was born on January 3, 1902, in a log cabin on Liberty Road near Northern Parkway in Baltimore County. I was the firstborn of eleven children. My father was working for a construction company in Howard Park, and they were building some very large buildings there."

- Ruth Elizabeth Rogers Dorsey, Interviewed by Louis S. Diggs, *Surviving in America*

"Our farmhouse was built in 1744, so it wasn't insulated nor was it built very [solidly]. Snow would blow in around the windows leaving a dusting on the windowsills. We had no running water on the upstairs, so at bedtime I would take a glass of water up to my bedroom...I slept [in the 1920s] with a heated flatiron wrapped in thick newspaper at the foot of my bed to keep my feet warm."

- Roay Ann McNamara, Seneca Creek / Middle River

"Most of the homes in Halethorpe have not changed in structure or appearance, although there are some of the new ranch-type homes scattered about. The main type of Victorian-era homes with their large yards and hedge or picket fences abound. Gone also are many of the early settlers who raised their large families in these lovely old homes. But with the passage of time, many of their grown children have now returned with children of their own to once again bring the soft lights and laughter to these homes.

- Joanna H. Coolahan, Halethorpe

"During World War II, I came to Middle River for work and I initially lived in an attic dorm with seven beds, and we ate in a dining hall. We paid rent by the week."

- Evan Bradey, Middle River Oral History Project

"During World War II, my sister, brother and I came to Baltimore County...It was a big change but I was excited...I had never seen an ice cream truck before...We lived in Trailer Site 1, near the Bengies. They had boardwalk-type sidewalks. At night we would have "blackouts" and we would run up to the utility building and have a party... we would listen to WITH radio."

- Marge and Ray Barhight, Middle River Oral History Project

"We took in boarders during World War II. There were so many boys around...they needed a place to stay so that's why so many people took in boarders. The boys were from all over – Tennessee, Pennsylvania, Virginia and the Carolinas."

- Ed and Emma Blazek, Middle River Oral History Project

"Martin's put up little four-room houses [during WWII]...They threw a dozen of them up in a day."

- Marie Bachman, Middle River Oral History Project

"After World War II, Martin's laid off all the engineers, so all of our neighbors were leaving Aero Acres and the houses were being sold off."

- Marge Katonka, Middle River Oral History Project

"Mars Estates was a great place to live and was a flourishing community [after World War II]. It was close to transportation and was quiet."

- Evan Bradey, Middle River Oral History Project

"It is not uncommon for sons and daughters to return and buy homes a few streets over from their parents."

- Richard Goth, Vice President, Relay Improvement Association

"I have always loved living here in Long Green, and I guess it is because it has been my home most of my life. I have nothing but good memories of life here in Long Green."
(Note: Mrs. Levere was born in Long Green on September 14, 1905)

- Marguerite Harvey Levere, Long Green

"Growing up and still living in the same 1905 house for over sixty years has made me who I am. My two brothers... share the same family property on Gun Road, above the old main line of the Baltimore and Ohio Railroad and the Patapsco River.

- Lucy W. McKean, Relay

"Irving J. Ensor was building houses on Northwood Drive and later on Gorsuch Road. I suppose that is when development really began.

- Claude (Greg) Gregory, Timonium

"There are beautiful houses and many places to see, like the Hampton Mansion."

- Lacey Parker, age 10, Lutherville

"Catonsville [is] the part of Baltimore County my family calls home. I was raised there, raised my own family there, began my business there. Real estate has ups and downs unlike Catonsville, which remains constant and strong. "Hometown USA on the edge of Big City USA."

- Joe Loverde, Catonsville

"I am still living in this house in good old Halethorpe... We had a wonderful life in Halethorpe."

- Teresa Breivogel, Halethorpe

"I have many very fond childhood memories from the time we lived in Baltimore County during the late 1950s and early 1960s. We lived on Fairbanks Road, which was a dead-end street. There were many young families in the neighborhood so there were plenty of children to play with after school and in the summer time... We played touch football, handball and baseball in the street or in our back yards, and there were always kids that would come outside and play. There was a small creek down behind the development and we often would catch crayfish in it. Woods bordered the development and there were very large beech trees that held more than one of our tree forts that we had built ourselves. Many wonderful hours were spent playing in the woods and the creek. In the winter, we could sled down the steep hill behind the houses."

- Jim Wharton, Mount Washington

"I have lived in Baltimore County since July 1938...the time has been the best of my life...I am proud to be considered a resident ... Baltimore County has not only beauty but fine living... most likely one of the best in Maryland, if not the entire United States."

- Johnna R. Suter, Sparks

"When I think of Baltimore County, I think of Dorothy from the Wizard of Oz: 'There's No Place Like Home'."

- April N. Goldring, Hereford

350

Chapter 3

Roads, Rivers & Rails

Traveling from Essex to Towson, or Lansdowne to Reisterstown, by automobile has been an excursion often measured in terms of minutes. Even with rush hour traffic and road construction in the equation, the trip does not consume a vast portion of the day. Thus, we often forget that when Baltimore County was founded, travel across the County was virtually impossible. At best, footpaths and later wagon trails were the extent of land-based travel and it could take days rather than minutes to reach a destination. Instead, the initial inhabitants relied more heavily on water transportation which is why the original areas of settlement were located in close proximity to the County's tidal rivers and the Chesapeake Bay.

The construction of roads was a major undertaking in terms of labor and expense and was accomplished largely by private entrepreneurs who built turnpikes and toll roads along with publicly funded roads and highways. Unpaved dirt roads and oyster shell paved roads eventually gave way to hard surfacing, but not until the twentieth century. Integrated with the system of roads, both horse-drawn and electric trolleys cars were progressions in the improvement of suburban transportation which connected Baltimore County and Baltimore City. The transition from horse power to gasoline power also dictated the need for improved roads. However, it was not until the opening of the Baltimore Beltway, in 1962, that it became easier to traverse the County. Routes I-95, I-795 and other major highways completed the network of more than 2360 miles of roads in the County.

Like road transportation, it is hard to overstate the impact of railroads on the development of the County. The Baltimore and Ohio railroad, the first in the country, ran its initial section of mainline through the area. Thus, the County was at the forefront of freight and passenger rail transportation. When the hundredth anniversary of railroading in America took place in 1927, it was a logical choice to have the Fair of the Iron Horse held in Baltimore County.

With the expansion of roads and rails, travel using boats proved less vital to the overall economy of the County, however, water and the control of water, with the construction of dams and reservoirs still contributed to the overall health of the region's economy in terms of commerce, natural resources and recreation.

Whether by roads, rivers or rails, transportation has always evoked a sense of freedom. There is nothing like the open road, riding the rails or being on the water. For personal transportation, commerce or for fun, mobility has and will be a way of life in Baltimore County.

"I travel not to go anywhere, but to go. I travel for travel's sake. The great affair is to move."

Robert Louis Stevenson

After the Revolutionary War, colonial roads had proven inadequate for the expanding traffic due to increased commerce and population. By the 1780s, the desire for better roads was a major issue in Baltimore County and gave impetus to the formation of turnpike companies. During the nineteenth century, almost twenty such roads were constructed. Tollhouses, like this one at Seven Mile Lane in Pikesville, were quite common along the privately owned turnpikes before the turn of the twentieth century. (Photograph courtesy of the Baltimore County Public Library)

A team of horses pulled a wagon up the hill leading into Spring Grove from Valley Road in Catonsville. The Spring Grove workers tended local fields and fresh produce and supplies were brought in for their subsistence. Other than the dirt road, this scene is almost the same after 110 years. (Photograph courtesy of the Catonsville Room, Baltimore County Public Library)

The graceful bridge connecting the Western Maryland Railroad train station to the Sudbrook Park development, circa 1900, was a testament to the way in which nature was used by the designer, Frederick Law Olmsted, to create aesthetically pleasing environments. Olmstead is best known for creating Central Park in New York City. (Photograph courtesy of the Baltimore County Public Library)

A Pimlico and Pikesville Railway horse car in the left middle distance waits for riders on Reisterstown Road near Walker Avenue in 1885. In the middle distance, a horse drawn bread wagon, owned by the Patapsco Flouring Company, part of the Charles Gambrill empire, is shown advertising Patapsco Baking Powder. The building behind the trees in the middle distance is the Burnt House Tavern. (Photograph courtesy of the Baltimore County Public Library)

In 1912, most Baltimore County residential streets were not yet paved. A view of "C" Street in Sparrows Point captured the transportation problems that occurred after a significant rain. However, wooden sidewalks were a welcome amenity for the pedestrian. *Note the First United Methodist Church on the right side of the street. (Photograph courtesy of the Dundalk-Patapsco Neck Historical Society)

By the early twentieth century, Baltimore County was aggressively paving its main roads. While the specific location is not known, penal labor assigned to Baltimore County public works projects assisted the laying of blacktop. A true steam roller can be seen in the foreground. (Photograph courtesy of the Baltimore County Public Library)

As automobiles slowly replaced horse-drawn vehicles, garages and gas stations quickly became thriving businesses. By 1921, "shade tree mechanics" were located in all parts of Baltimore County. This building served as Peter's Garage in two different locations in Catonsville for more than thirty years. *Note the gravity-fed gas pumps. (Photograph courtesy of the Baltimore County Public Library)

This unique bus was used during World War II on the Q Line, the route between Halethorpe and Baltimore City, to carry the large number of workers from the southwest area of Baltimore County to the Westinghouse plant on Wilkens Avenue. (Photograph courtesy of Paul E. Dimler)

Post World War II Towson, in 1951, was still quite rural as demonstrated by the view of York Road, looking south, near the subsequent construction site of the Quality Inn. The Church of the Immaculate Conception and the old Towson water tower are seen at the crest of the hill. (Photograph courtesy of the Baltimore County Public Library)

The Parkville loop was a center of transportation where streetcars, buses and automobiles converged in 1952. (Photograph courtesy of the Greater Parkville Community Council History Committee)

In 1906, the No. 26 street car line was started between Sparrows Point and Baltimore City. While the line was always successful, gas rationing during World War II caused its use to be at an all time high. The photo was taken in 1957 from the old Fort Holabird railroad bridge spanning Dundalk Avenue. The integration of automobile and rail traffic was apparent. St. Timothy's Lutheran Church is seen in the background. (Photograph courtesy of C. H. Echols)

By the mid-1950s, traffic was a growing concern in many Baltimore County urban areas. York Road, viewed south to north, was just an example of this dilemma for county officials. (Photograph courtesy of Jacques Kelly)

To keep pace with industrial and urban growth, the Baltimore Beltway was constructed as part of the Interstate System under the National System of Interstate and Defense Highways, during the Eisenhower Administration in 1956. The ceremony opening of the original thirty miles of the Beltway took place on July 27, 1962. A group of vehicles lined up to be the first vehicles to travel the Beltway. (Photograph courtesy of Jacques Kelly)

The Perring Parkway intersection with the Beltway was just being completed when this aerial photograph was taken in June of 1962. The Satyr Hill Shopping Center is at the center and Joppa Road is above the commercial area. (Photograph courtesy of Jacques Kelly)

The May 19, 1974 sign declared that the Exxon Station at York and Bosley Roads was closed due to the gas crisis. (Photograph courtesy of the Baltimore County Public Library)

Named for Francis Scott Key, the Key Bridge opened in 1977. The structure, 8,636 feet in length, is part of the Baltimore Beltway (695) and crosses the Patapsco River from Hawkins Point to Sollers Point. The original cost of the bridge was in excess of $50 million. (Photograph courtesy of the Baltimore County Public Library)

Ever improving the network of roads in Baltimore County, this ceremony marked the grand opening of the extension of Maryland Route 43 in Middle River. The 3.8 mile extension, from White Marsh to Eastern Boulevard, was central to the renaissance of eastern Baltimore. This project demonstrated the connection between the development of roads and business development; a relationship which has occurred over Baltimore County's 350 year history. (Photograph courtesy of the Baltimore County Office of Communications)

Rivers

Before the era of air conditioning, local rivers provided a way in which to get cool on hot summer days. Dorothy Baldwin, Erin C.W. Davis, George Rogers and George Blackman Davis enjoyed the Gunpowder River, circa the 1890s. (Photograph courtesy of the Baltimore County Public Library)

Throughout Baltimore County, the significant number of rivers and streams made bridge construction necessary as the network of roads increased during the first part of the twentieth century. One example of this construction was the new, concrete Glen Arm Road Bridge at Cromwell Bridge Road, over the Gunpowder River, circa the 1920s. (Photograph courtesy of the Baltimore County Public Library)

The Loch Raven Bridge, No. 1, casts a perfect reflection in the tranquil waters. The date of the photograph is unknown. (Photograph courtesy of the Historical Society of Baltimore County)

A lone fisherman cast his line in front of the spillway of Lake Roland Dam during the 1930s. (Photograph courtesy of the Baltimore County Public Library)

Prettyboy Dam, located in the Hereford area, was completed in 1932. The fountain made a spectacular site in 1933 as the dam impounded the Gunpowder Falls to create a reservoir of nineteen billion gallons of water. The Prettyboy Dam and Loch Raven Dam currently provide sixty-one percent of the drinking water for the Baltimore metropolitan area. (Photograph courtesy of the Stiffler sisters)

The Bunker Hill Covered Bridge, on Bunker Hill Road, crossed the Gunpowder River near Hereford and portrayed a more simplistic way of life in Baltimore County. The original bridge was built in 1880 and was rebuilt after a fire in 1961. Unfortunately, the bridge no longer exists due to a second fire caused by arson in 1971. (Photograph courtesy of the Historical Society of Baltimore County)

Surviving hurricane Agnes, Avalon Dam, on the Patapsco, upstream from the Thomas Viaduct, was still a good place to fish in the late 1970s. (Photograph courtesy of Maryland Department of Natural Resources)

The Glenn L. Martin Maryland Aviation Museum hosted the 4th Annual Baltimore County Community Waterfront Festival on May 10, 2008 at the Lockheed Martin property along Dark Head Cove and on Wilson Point Road in Middle River, Maryland. The event celebrated the heritage and the fun of living on or near the water. (Photograph courtesy of the Baltimore County Office of Communications)

Peter Cooper's Tom Thumb was the first steam-powered locomotive operated by the B&O railroad. In 1831, the locomotive not actually named until forty years later, was clocked at making the trip from Ellicott's Mills to Baltimore City in just fifty-seven minutes. This replica of the Tom Thumb was built for the 1927 Fair of the Iron Horse and was in rehearsal for a television show in the mid-1950s as the train traveled over the original mainline through Lansdowne, Halethorpe, Arbutus and Relay. (Photograph courtesy of James P. Gallagher and Greenberg Publishing Company, Inc.)

The B&O Railroad took this unique photograph of their promotional department taking a photograph of the Royal Blue steaming through southwest Baltimore County near Halethorpe at the turn of the twentieth century. The trees and the vegetation demonstrate how rural the area was along the original B&O mainline. (Photograph courtesy of Barnard, Roberts and Co., Inc.)

A group of children sit on a bank with their teacher at the Sudbrook Station and wait for the Western Maryland Railroad. It is thought that the children were on a fieldtrip and were ready to head back to Baltimore City, circa 1900. (Photograph courtesy of the Baltimore County Public Library)

Brooklandville Station, located on Falls Road is an excellent example of a turn-of-the-century railroad station. With the other stations on the Northern Central main line and its Green Spring Branch, this station was instrumental in promoting significant suburban and estate development based on "commuter" railroad service until 1933. (Photograph courtesy of John McGrain and the Historical Society of Baltimore County)

Railroad workers gather for a photograph at the Gwynnbrook Station, circa 1900. (Photograph courtesy of the Historical Society of Baltimore County)

The historic William Mason was a featured locomotive at the Fair of the Iron Horse. (Photograph courtesy of William Hollifield)

BALTIMORE AND OHIO RAILROAD
1827 Centenary 1927
THE
FAIR OF THE IRON HORSE
SEATS MUST BE VACATED IMMEDIATELY
AFTER CLOSE OF MORNING PAGEANT

11 A. M.
PAGEANT
SATURDAY
OCTOBER
1927 15
CENTER STAND

The Fair of the Iron Horse, in the fall of 1927, was the 100th anniversary celebration of railroading. Sponsored by the B&O Railroad, the extravaganza cost over one million dollars. (Graphics courtesy of Dr. Barry A. Lanman)

"Milestones
(at "The Fair of the Iron Horse".
Baltimore, September 24 to October 8)

Chief Two Guns White Calf appeared at the Fair of the Iron Horse with several members of the Blood and Pigeon Tribes of the Blackfoot Nation from Montana's Glacier Park. The Native Americans were the most popular attraction at the Fair. (Photograph courtesy of William Hollifield)

A cavalcade of locomotives, rolling stock, floats, horses, oxen, mules and 500 costumed actors, along with many other attractions, were part of a two hour show called the Pageant of the Iron Horse. It was estimated that over 1,500,000 visitors witnessed the Fair and the Pageant. (Photograph courtesy of William Hollifield)

A Ma & Pa steam train approached the Glen Arm station on April 18, 1946. In just a few short years, steam locomotives gave way to the more efficient and cleaner-burning diesel locomotives. (Photograph courtesy of the Historical Society of Baltimore County)

This diesel was festively painted for the celebration of the Millennium and operated in the Dundalk area. The locomotive represents that railroad transportation is still a major part of the economy in Baltimore County. Along with the transportation of freight, Amtrack and the light rail system provide passenger transportation for the County citizens. (Photograph courtesy of Bill Barry, Director of Labor Studies, CCBC Dundalk campus)

Since 1992, the Light Rail has traveled from Hunt Valley to the heart of Baltimore City. By 2008, over 27,000 trips were made each business day. Thus, this public system of transportation provides a way for Baltimore County residents to support the "Green" initiative. (Photograph courtesy of the Office of Economic Development)

Baltimore County Memories . . .

"Travel during this era (late eighteenth century) before development of private turnpikes could be dangerous and time consuming. A trip from Hampton Mansion, just north of Towson, to Baltimore could take from seven to nine hours, depending on the conditions of the road."

- Neal A. Brooks, Eric G. Rokel and William C. Hughs, *A History of Baltimore County*

"For centuries, farmers relied on the working farm horse to help grow their food and provide their transportation. The Old York Road became a direct connection from Baltimore City to York Pennsylvania, cutting through the middle of Baltimore County. The dirt highway was used by the citizens in carriage, wagon, or riding atop the all-important horse. The road still retains its uphill curves, which eased the horse's work when pulling a heavy load."

- Janey Mowell, Glencoe

"My parents had their own horse and buggy, and it gave me some of my best remembrances of my life in Foote's Hill. My dad would take us in the horse and buggy all over the countryside in northern Baltimore County. It was so wonderful to be able to enjoy seeing all the beautiful sights in the countryside."

- Mabel Janet Smith, Northern Baltimore County

"Once a community decided that it needed to up-grade its hand-drawn fire equipment, the condition of the roads became an important factor. Records and photographs indicate that two-horse hitches were all that was required, even in hilly areas. When motor-driven apparatus became the norm, after 1912, attention was still given to the width and solidity of roadways: Apparatus needed to be light in weight, have 6 cylinder engines for speed, and be easy to maintain. American-LaFrance became the manufacturer of choice."

- Stephen G. Heaver, Director & Curator, Fire Museum of Maryland

"Two bells from the conductor and off we went to the next stop. The Dundalk stop where more mill men piled on. The trolley's air compressor throbbing hard like it couldn't wait to get rolling. The tall silver-haired motorman turned the shiny black knob with his big gloved hand and off we went full speed. Down the steel rails we rolled. A good breeze through the partly opened window bringing the tar smell from the tracks. The motorman jamming his right foot hard on the metal plunger making the whistle scream out a warning. Clear the tracks. Full load. No more stops. We're coming through."

- Ben Herman, *Red Trolley Days*

"In the early part of the 1920s, there was a need to build the Loch Raven Reservoir. A tiny town my ancestors had lived in, by the name of Warren, had to be flooded. When Loch Raven Reservoir's water is [down legend says] you can still see the Warren's schoolhouse flagpole from the Warren Road bridge."

- Betty Tracey Chenoweth, Ruxton

"When I was little, I thought Halethorpe was the end of the world. First Avenue had a dead end and still does, so I believed the world ended at the very end of First Avenue. Walking home from school, looking at the beautiful hills of Relay, I pictured myself as Heidi, living in the valley."

- Edith L. Foxwell, Halethorpe

"York Road was a two-lane country road in the 1930s. Scouts from Troop 319, Hunt's Church in Riderwood, assisted in parking cars during the Timonium State Fair at the Timonium Fair Grounds. The area east of York Road, opposite the Fairgrounds, was still an operating farm...An auto trip north of Cockeysville, on York Road,

could be a chore... and if you were behind a tractor trailer it was slow going. This was before I-83. About 1948, construction began on I-83. It consisted of only two lanes north and south of Beaver Dam Road."

- Claude "Greg" Gregory, Timonium

"Because of the proximity of Halethorpe to Baltimore and because several means of transportation were available, people from the area had easy access to Baltimore City."

- Louis S. Diggs, *Surviving in America*

"My sisters and I shared the attic bedroom, and in the summer you slept with the windows open as there was no air conditioning and it was hot. At night besides all of the summer noises like the crickets and frogs, you could also hear the ships' whistles from the inner harbor, at least until the beltway went in (mid 1960s) and then you could hear the traffic. You could also hear the truck coming up the street at night to spray for mosquitoes--Lord, quick close the window or it would spray in!"

- Nancy Eubert, Parkville, Carney and Cub Hill

"When the beltway was constructed, it opened up transportation to more remote locations of the county. It was a 'Sunday adventure' when all the neighborhood kids would pile into the sedan and better if someone had a station wagon, since there were no seat belt laws back then, to ride to the 'end of the beltway'."

- Lynn Sklar, Towson/Parkville

"My girlfriend Kathy and I would ride the bus into Dundalk and go to the Strand to see a movie all by ourselves – we felt very grown-up because we were only ten years old at the time. The entire escapade would cost under a dollar."

- Jean Bennett, Dundalk

"Every year on 4th of July, my parents packed their cars with picnic goodies along with all the children, twelve in total, and headed to Double Rock Park. The children would run to the stream and play while the parents decorated the picnic area."

- Susan Ward Hahn, Govans/Parkville

"I grew up in Edgemere and graduated from Sparrows Point High in 1979. Edgemere is a water-oriented community…My favorite memory is ice skating on the frozen river at Greenhill Cove off Lynch Point. Hundreds of people came from miles around…and neighbors would offer their piers to access the frozen tributary to Back River and the Chesapeake Bay. We would skate and play pick-up hockey games…At dusk, we would build bonfires right on the ice and skate under the stars.

- Terry Sage, Edgemere

I have lived in Relay for over sixty years and I rode one of the last passenger trains on the old main line of the Baltimore and Ohio Railroad from Avalon Station to Baltimore when I was a young girl. Now the trains haul only cargo, but I still love to hear their whistle."

- Lucy W. McKean, Relay

"I love the fact that, on any given day, the kids and I can pack a lunch, hop in the car and be at the beach in twenty minutes from our home in Essex."

- Lisa Morris, Essex

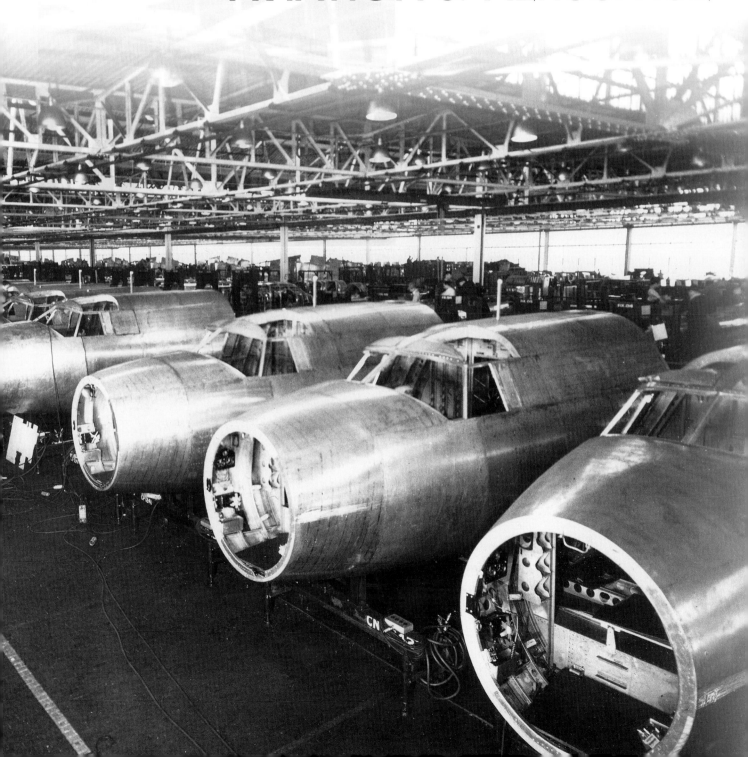

Chapter 4

AVIATION & AEROSPACE

*F*rom biplanes to rockets, Baltimore County has been involved in the development of aviation and aerospace since the early days of powered flight. Like mills, ironworks and steel production, the industry of aviation has been of paramount importance to the economic health of Baltimore County.

While the Wright Brothers historic flight occurred in 1903, the first public exhibition of the airplane did not transpire until 1908 at Ft. Myer, Virginia. Just two years later, Baltimore County found itself on the international stage with the Baltimore Aero Meet of 1910 and the first flight over a city by a planned route. Following these initial events, several permanent facilities were constructed in the County after World War I. Logan Field and Harbor Field were two of these major centers for aviation.

In the 1930s, airmail and passenger services were initiated in Baltimore County along with the development of a seaplane terminal; a concept that failed to live up to its promise. While these were noteworthy events, the construction of the Glenn L. Martin Company on 1260 acres in Middle River would be the most significant factor positioning Baltimore County as a major producer of airplanes during World War II. The Martin B-26 Marauder and the Baltimore were just two of the aircraft that would build a reputation for the company and its home town.

With the end of the war, private and commercial aviation once again flourished and small airstrips like Rutherford Field became local centers of private aviation. However, with the development of the Cold War, following World War II, the Nike Missile Program for defense was established and the Glenn L. Martin Company participated in the development of various rockets such as Vanguard and Mace. After the sale of the Glenn L. Martin Company, Middle River Aero Systems continued the manufacturing tradition initiated by Glenn L. Martin.

Thus, nearly a century of aviation and aerospace history can be traced from the first flights over Halethorpe to the flights of Baltimore County's hometown astronauts such as Captain Robert L. Curbeam, Jr. To secure this aspect of Baltimore County's rich heritage, the Glenn L. Martin Maryland Aviation Museum was formed. The museum not only preserves vital artifacts, it chronicles the County's human contributions to aviation and aerospace.

"When once you have tasted flight, you will forever walk the earth with your eyes turned skyward, for there you have been, and there you will always long to return."

Leonardo da Vinci

The Baltimore Aero Meet of 1910 was the third such air show in the United States and occurred only two years after the first public exhibition of flight which was held at Ft. Myers, Virginia. An estimated 50,000 witnessed this demonstration of flight at the Halethorpe field in November, 1910. The Aero Meet attracted some of the best aviators in the world including Charles Foster Willard, Count Jacques de Lesseps, Hubert Latham, James Radley, J. Armstrong Drexel, Clifford Harmon, Eugene Ely and Glen Curtiss. The aviators competed for cash prizes and gave demonstrations. While the Wright Brothers briefly attended the show, they sent Archibald "Arch" Hoxsey to compete with the Wright Flyer. (Photograph courtesy of Dr. Barry A. Lanman)

HUBERT LATHAM IN HIS ANTOINETTE MONOPLANE, STARTING ON HIS FLIGHT at HALETHORPE NEAR BALTO. MD.

While the contests, demonstrations and exhibits at the Baltimore Aero Meet of 1910 were highly successful and well received, one flight stood apart from the rest: A flight over Baltimore City. Hubert Latham was selected to attempt the historic flight. (Photograph courtesy of Dr. Barry A. Lanman)

The first flight over a city by a
planned route was designed so that the
largest audience could witness the historic event. It was estimated that hundreds
of thousands of people may have seen Hubert
Latham's historic flight on November 7, 1910.
(Map courtesy of *The Sun*)

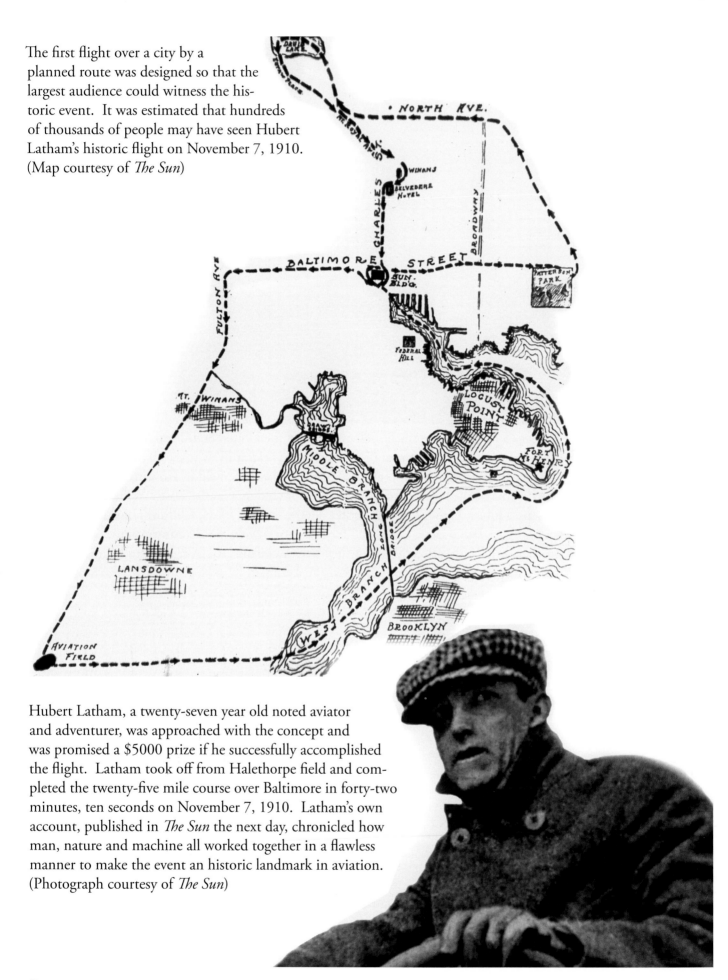

Hubert Latham, a twenty-seven year old noted aviator
and adventurer, was approached with the concept and
was promised a $5000 prize if he successfully accomplished
the flight. Latham took off from Halethorpe field and completed the twenty-five mile course over Baltimore in forty-two
minutes, ten seconds on November 7, 1910. Latham's own
account, published in *The Sun* the next day, chronicled how
man, nature and machine all worked together in a flawless
manner to make the event an historic landmark in aviation.
(Photograph courtesy of *The Sun*)

This drawing printed in *The Sun* on November 8, 1910 was entitled "The Modern Age" and it depicted Baltimore County on the cutting edge of technology. (Drawing courtesy of *The Sun*)

Logan Field, in Dundalk, was the center of aviation activity by 1918. Numerous biplanes flew into Logan Field for this event. (Photograph courtesy of the Dundalk -Patapsco Neck Historical Society)

C. T. Luddington founded the Luddington Air Line which began service between Washington, Baltimore, Philadelphia and New York on November, 24, 1930. A passenger on the first flight was Amelia Earhart who was a Vice President of the company. In 1933, the company merged into what became Eastern Airlines. The airline flew out of Logan Field in Dundalk. (Photograph courtesy of the Baltimore County Public Library)

Corporal Ned Martini with pilot D.F.A. Joyce and postal employee J. Cameron Coleman prepared to meet the first mail plane from the south at Logan Field. The man in the passenger seat of the open cockpit plane is handing out the mail sacks. (Photograph courtesy of the Baltimore County Public Library)

The arrival of the first Pan Am Clipper seaplane, circa 1937, attracted a huge crowd of curious spectators and the local media. Standing in front of the WFBR radio station mobile van were, from left to right, Gladys Marsbeck, Virginia Echols, Louise Chell and Antionette Chell. Seaplanes were to have become the future wave of aviation, however, that did not materialize. (Photograph courtesy of the Dundalk-Patapsco Neck Historical Society)

A Pan American Airlines Bermuda Clipper was perched on the loading dock, circa 1939, at Harbor Field preparing for a flight. A round-trip fare to Bermuda, in 1939, cost $100. The area is now Dundalk Marine Terminal. (Photograph courtesy of the Dundalk-Patapsco Neck Historical Society)

Moving to Baltimore County in 1928, Glenn L. Martin bought over 1260 acres in the suburb of Middle River and built some of the most modern aircraft manufacturing facilities of its time. The Glenn L. Martin Company produced over 80 different types of aircraft totaling more than 11,000 planes. Before its merger with Lockheed in 1995, the company also produced missiles and aerospace components. Plant #1 is shown in 1940 and is now Middle River Aero Systems. (Photograph courtesy of the Glenn L. Martin Maryland Aviation Museum)

This Glen L. Martin airplane carried the name of its hometown; the Baltimore. Several of the planes were in final assembly at Plant #1 during World War II. *Note the British Insignia. (Photograph courtesy of the Glenn L. Martin Maryland Aviation Museum)

An impressive array of B-26 Marauders were lined up in the sub-assembly line, C Building, in 1944, at the Glenn L. Martin plant. Glenn L. Martin, like many other defense contractors, greatly contributed to the war effort. (Photograph courtesy of the Baltimore County Public Library)

A large crowd gathered around a troop carrier command plane after a U.S. Army show at the Municipal Airport in Dundalk. The event occurred at the very end of World War II on May 6, 1945. (Photograph courtesy of the Baltimore County Public Library)

The last of 4056 B-26 Marauders was posed in front of the terminal building at the Martin Factory Airport now Martin State Airport. (Photograph courtesy of the Glenn L. Martin Maryland Aviation Museum)

In the 1950s, due to the demand for passenger flights, commercial airliners replaced military airplanes on the runway at Martin Airport. (Photograph courtesy of the Baltimore County Public Library)

Built between 1951 and 1956, the B-57 Canberra, was used during Vietnam as a conventional bomber. The B-57 was also used as a nuclear weapons platform. (Photograph courtesy of the Glenn L. Martin Maryland Aviation Museum)

The Martin P5M, in the background, had been produced during the late 1950s and was replaced by the P6M, which was the last aircraft designed for the Glenn L. Martin Company. (Photograph courtesy of the Glenn L. Martin Maryland Aviation Museum)

Due to political tensions that led to the Cold War, Glenn L. Martin was contracted in 1946 to develop the Matador missile, based on the German V-1 buzz bombs. The TM-64 Mace (shown here) was derived from the Matador. Both were in operation and deployed until 1960. (Photograph courtesy of the Glenn L. Martin Maryland Aviation Museum)

John Pinkerton served on this 747 along with an earlier 707 while assigned to the elite crew of Air Force One between 1980 and 1992.   (Photograph courtesy of John Pinkerton)

John Pinkerton, a Halethorpe resident is shown with President Reagan. Pinkerton was a flight engineer on Air Force One, serving Presidents, members of Congress and members of the Cabinet. (Photograph courtesy of John Pinkerton)

A veteran of three space flights, Captain Robert L. Curbeam, Jr. returned from a twelve day mission on the Space Shuttle Discovery to the International Space Station in December, 2006. Curbeam, who grew up in Woodlawn, graduated from Woodlawn High School, received a diploma from the Naval Academy and served as a Topgun Pilot before becoming an astronaut. (Photograph courtesy of the Baltimore County Office of Communications)

The fascination of flight is seen on the faces of both father and child. (Photograph courtesy of the Baltimore County Office of Communications)

Baltimore County Memories . . .

"The Baltimore Aero Meet of 1910, held in Halethorpe, was referred to as 'an epoch in practical aviation and to that date, the largest audience of the world had witnessed a single performance of aviation'."
- **Book of the Royal Blue**, December 1910

"Hubert Latham made the first flight over a city on November 7, 1910, when he took off from the Baltimore Aero Meet of 1910 in Halethorpe, flew over Baltimore City and returned to Halethorpe. After this historic flight, he simply stated: "In a word, as you Americans put it: It was 'great'.""
- **Hubert Latham, *The Sun*, December 8, 1910**

"My living in Baltimore County affords me the necessities to travel and shop on a daily basis. However, most importantly, living here allowed me easy access to the Baltimore Air Park where I was a pilot, since 1928 and owned an aircraft and a hanger there. However, in 1980 the air park was turned into a housing development of over 700 homes.
- **George Levis, Dundalk**

"I worked hard at Martin's to get the planes out because people were killing our boys."
- **Marge Katonka, Middle River Oral History Project**

"I requested the Martin B-26 Marauder and never regretted the decision…it was my favorite aircraft… The Marauder provided challenges and experience during WWII that prepared me for a successful Air Force career."
- **Les Dunning, Colonel U.S.A.F., Retired**

"We had a sense of hands-on commitment to the war effort. A B-26 flew over the airport and it was a sense of pride knowing that we had a hand in building that plane."
- **Virginia Atkinson, Middle River Oral History Project**

"In this area, the B-26 was something special…It was like they were all your children."
- **Marge and Ray Barhight, Middle River Oral History Project**

"One interesting thing was the D Building of the Martin Company…they [built] seaplanes during World War II as well as bombers and the PBM. The seaplanes would come down off the ramp into that lagoon and taxi out to the Bay, and then takeoff on their test flights. Many times I went canoeing out there and got overturned by the waves from the seaplanes… I remember the Mars Flying Boat – it was the largest seaplane ever built."
- **Carol Dick, Middle River Oral History Project**

"I won a recognition award for service…after five years with Martin's. The ceremony was the happiest night of my life."
- **Marge Katonka, Middle River Oral History Project**

"People at Martin's came from all over...integration was a gradual process."

- Minerva Gordon, Middle River Oral History Project

"After World War II, I was discharged from the service at Ft. Meade. I worked briefly in the engineering department at Martin's in the heating and ventilating section. One of the projects I worked on was a system of putting fresh air between the two windshields in the pilots' cabin of the aircraft. They were having a lot of trouble at that time on the propeller-driven planes with birds that would strike the windshield and cause it to shatter. They thought that was due to the difference in the temperature between inside and outside. One of the thrilling experiments I devised was thrusting frozen chickens with compressed air at airplane windshields with different temperatures inside and outside."

- Charles "Bill" Springer, Parkville

"Both my father, Harry Adler, and my grandfather, Charles Adler, Jr., flew small private airplanes in the 1940s and 50s. [My father] owned a private airplane, which he kept at the Curtis Wright Airport on Smith Avenue in the Pikesville area. Before radar was used in small planes, you flew by 'sight.' So when he left the Wright Airport one day and headed out for a ride, he knew that when he turned around to come back, his 'landmark' for the airport was a quarry located on Greenspring Avenue. He flew for a while...and noticed that his fuel was getting low. He turned around and soon after saw a quarry. Thinking that this was his landmark, he started looking for a landing strip. Soon he saw one and landed. Unfortunately this was not the Wright Airport, but one in Cockeysville, quite a few miles from home."

- Susan A. Davis, Pikesville

"An aviation division of the Maryland National Guard was formed in 1921 and designated the 29th Division Aviation, which flew JN-4s ('Jennies') borrowed from the Army Air Service and flew at Logan Field in Dundalk, where Dundalk village now stands... This squadron was also the first Guard unit to practice live parachute jumps, and by summer of 1926, five successful jumps had been made... At an event held on October 26, 1925, at Bay Shore Park on the Chesapeake Bay, Lieutenant Jimmy Doolittle broke the world's speed record at 232.573 mph in a Curtis Racer to win the Schneider Cup race for the United States. Writer John F. R. Scott attests to its being 'one in a series of events which were to make the State of Maryland a leader in the development of military and commercial aviation... Harbor Field, originally Municipal Airport, opened near Dundalk on November 16, 1941, replacing Logan Field for scheduled airline operations in the region until being replaced by Friendship International Airport in June 1950. It was also the home for the 104th Fighter Squadron of the Maryland Air National Guard from summer of 1946 until July 1955'."

- John Scott, Jr., *Voyages into Airy Regions*

"There are two airfields in the vicinity [of Perry Hall. One of the airfields was located] on Ferguson Road, a private field, was started on the Spamer farm in 1947 as a landing field for their own plane. Gradually other local owners of small craft housed their planes there. Sky diving at this field is a colorful event on weekends.

- Carroll Dunn, History of the Perry Hall Improvement Association

"The Glenn L. Martin Maryland Aviation Museum, located at Martin State Airport, reminds us of the historical significance this place and our citizens played as part of the history of our country."

- Joseph Bartenfelder, Baltimore County Councilman, 6th District

Chapter 5

AGRICULTURE & EQUESTRIAN LIFE

350
YEARS
BALTIMORE
COUNTY
MARYLAND
1659-2009

*E*xploring the twenty-first century communities of Arbutus, Essex, Perry Hall, Towson or Woodlawn is a study in urbanization. However, traveling further north on Route 83 towards Pennsylvania, the open expanse of land that still exists is reflective of Baltimore County's agrarian and equestrian heritage.

Supporting hunting and gathering, initial crops in Baltimore County were grown by settlers for their sustenance. It was a life of simple sufficiency. However, corn, wheat, tobacco and other products became the cash crops necessary to create an economy. Because agricultural production was such a labor intensive endeavor, the demand for workers was insatiable. Thus, convict labor, indentured servants and slaves were viewed as a solution to a paid workforce. Such practices continued for the first two centuries of Baltimore County's history. However, the end of slavery after the Civil War and the development of labor saving devices such as the steel plow, mechanical reapers and the use of steam power by the late 1800s dramatically reduced the need for manual labor. While the advent of the gasoline powered tractor continued to revolutionize Baltimore County farms, increased productivity was both an economic blessing and a curse due to the concepts of supply and demand.

Not until the beginning of the twentieth century did agriculture lose its status as the economic engine that drove the Baltimore County economy. Today, less than 1% of the economy in Baltimore County is based on agriculture. Yet the jurisdiction still contains a vast amount of land untouched by urban or industrial development. Issues such as green technology and conservation of land for future generations are but two of the topics that will impact the future of Baltimore County's remaining agricultural acreage.

Like agriculture, equestrian life is an enduring part of Baltimore County's history; both were intertwined for practical as well as recreational reasons. While the pre-twentieth century demand for horsepower on farms was self-explanatory, for the gentry, horses were also part of the social setting and key for fox hunts, horse racing and other social events. In contemporary Baltimore County, Legacy Chase is an occasion that combines the tradition of equestrian life while raising large sums of money for worthwhile causes. Such endeavors extend the equestrian legacy into the twenty-first century.

"Cultivators of the earth are the most valuable citizens. They are the most vigorous, the most independent, the most virtuous, and they are tied to their country and wedded to it's liberty and interests by the most lasting bands."

Thomas Jefferson

"No hour of life is wasted that is spent in the saddle."

Winston Churchill

Grain harvesting in the 1880s was a major event and took a great deal of manual labor which included most members of the family. This harvest scene was taken on the Charles G. Snavely farm off Bottom Road southeast of Baldwin. Most of the men were from surrounding farms and helped each other harvest their crops. *Note the wooden cradles and rakes. (Photograph courtesy of the Baltimore County Public Library)

A pre-World War I harvest in Reisterstown demonstrated that farming was still a family business and required a great deal of manual labor. (Photograph courtesy of the Historical Society of Baltimore County)

African American farm workers operated a reaper, drawn by a four-horse team on the Zephaniah Poteet farm in Mt. Pleasant in Cockeysville. The production of grain in Baltimore County was a significant commodity in the nineteenth and early twentieth centuries. As compared to the manual harvesting of grain, this reaper was a major labor-saving device. (Photograph courtesy of the Baltimore County Public Library)

A two horse team, in 1912, pulled a hand plow guided by a Lutherville farmer in much the same manner as it had been done during the majority of the nineteenth century. (Photograph courtesy of the Baltimore County Public Library)

Steam power mechanized farming and increased production just in time for the increased demand for food caused by World War I. Frank Kalb of Woodlawn was at the wheel of his Peerless steam tractor and thresher. (Photograph courtesy of the Baltimore County Public Library)

Had the Guinness Book of World Records been in existence in 1903, this Sparrows Point field of corn might have captured top honors for the tallest stalks. By the height of the adult gentlemen, it appears that the corn was at least thirteen feet tall. (Photograph courtesy of the Dundalk-Patapsco Neck Historical Society)

Grace Councilman Hoen, standing in a white dress, was paying child asparagus pickers at Bloomfield in Glyndon, circa 1912. (Photograph courtesy of the Baltimore County Public Library)

Before modern electronics, this classic farm bell was used to summon workers for meals. The bell was photographed on Connemara Farm, 10598 Beaver Dam Road, Cockeysville, by John McGrain, County Historian. (Photograph courtesy of John McGrain and the Historical Society of Baltimore County)

The Brooklandwood Dairy at Emerson Farms in Brooklandville, was established by Bromo-Seltzer inventor, Isaac Emerson, in 1913. The dairy operated for forty years and was popular with the public for its natural dairy products. (Photograph courtesy of Jacques Kelly)

Sheaves of grain were stacked under protective covers to keep out moisture until the arrival of the thresher. This field was near Hereford and was most likely photographed from York Road in the 1920s. (Photograph courtesy of the Baltimore County Public Library)

The Shane Homemakers Club worked to-gether to make a cauldron of apple butter during the Depression. The activity was a necessity as well as a social event. The Club met at the Shane International Order of Odd Fellows Hall on Oakenshaw Road. (Photograph courtesy of the Baltimore County Public Library)

In 1976, the Meadowdale barn located on Belfast Road was still in use and looked as it did when it was first built by Lewis M. Bacon in 1893. *Note the ventilating cupolas which were estheti-cally pleasing as well as highly functional. (Photograph courtesy of the Baltimore County Public Library)

The S. M. Elder property was located at Beckleysville and Falls Road. It appeared to be typical of Baltimore County farms near the end of the De-pression. (Photograph cour-tesy of the Baltimore County Public Library)

In 1987, Harriet Maginess drove a McCormick Farmall tractor on the family farm in White Hall. Even with such equipment, agriculture was still a family affair. (Photograph courtesy of the Baltimore County Public Library)

James Chilcoat demonstrated a grain cradle at the Historical Society of Baltimore County in 1975. Chilcoat was the last superintendent of the Alms House for Baltimore County, the current location of the Historical Society. (Photograph courtesy of the Baltimore County Public Library)

Highly mechanized farm equipment has taken a great deal of the physical burden out of farming. However, the costs of equipment and expenses, the increased value of the land and the encroachment of commercial and residential development have been just a few of the factors that have threatened agricultural development in Baltimore County. In 2008, the USDA Natural Resources Conservation Service provided Baltimore County with $1.6 million in matching funds under the Farm and Ranch Land Protection Program to purchase conservation easements. (Photograph courtesy of the Baltimore County Office of Communications)

Raising the next generation of Baltimore County residents, who will care for the environment, is a priority. Participation in parades is just one way in which to get children involved in environmental or "green" issues impacting the future. (Photograph courtesy of the Baltimore County Office of Communications)

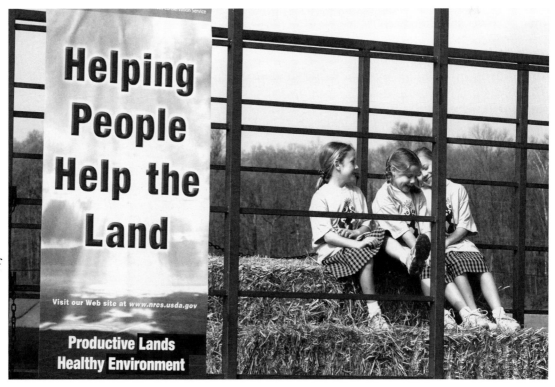

Equestrian Life

The Devon Horse Show, held in the southwest area of Baltimore County during May of 1890, was a major equestrian event. Colonel Edward Morrell, in top hat and holding a buggy whip, is on the "box" of his four-in-hand with Fanny Lurman. The dress denoted the formality of this event. (Photograph courtesy of the Baltimore County Public Library)

The Towson Horse Company was located in the area of east Pennsylvania Avenue in Towson. Livery stables were an important service in the early twentieth century before the horseless carriage became the major source of transportation. (Photograph courtesy of the Baltimore County Public Library)

The grandeur of estate living in Baltimore County was captured in this professional photograph of Theodore Lurman taken in September, 1886 at Farmlands. Catonsville High School is now the site of Farmlands and part of the campus houses the Lurman Theater named in honor of the original owner. (Photograph courtesy of the Catonsville Room, Baltimore County Public Library)

Throughout the history of the Timonium Fair, horse racing has been a major part of the events. This race took place in 1908. (Photograph courtesy of the Baltimore County Public Library)

The Towson Ice Company, like most businesses in 1912, was transitioning between horse-drawn wagons and motorized trucks. In this era, ice was manufactured in Baltimore City and transported to Towson in the Packard truck (left). Home deliveries were still being made by horse and wagon. By 1920, Clayton Seitz began manufacturing ice in Towson. (Photograph courtesy of the Baltimore County Public Library)

Foxhunting throughout Baltimore County was a sport associated with the upper class. A joint meeting of the Elkridge Hounds and the Green Spring Valley Hounds took place at Hampton Mansion in 1913. (Photograph courtesy of the Baltimore County Public Library)

Sagamore Farms, owned by Alfred G. Vanderbilt, was one of the most successful Thoroughbred breeding farms in the mid-Atlantic region during the mid-twentieth century. Discovery and Native Dancer were among the champion horses raised at Sagamore Farms. (Photograph courtesy of the Baltimore County Public Library)

Mark Marian was a highly successful African American trainer of horses in Baltimore County. (Photograph courtesy of Louis Diggs)

In order to save the land at the entrance of Greenspring Valley, in the mid-1990s, Pedie Killebrew conceived the idea of Shawn Downs, the Legacy Chase, Children's Fair and the Vendor Village in order to raise funds to purchase the land. After years of work, she and twelve founding partners were able to purchase the property and create one of the finest equestrian facilities in the state of Maryland. The Legacy Chase now boasts attendance of around 16,000 spectators annually, making it the largest and most successful of the Maryland Steeplechases. Each year, the races and other events create gifts of over $170,000 for local charities. (Photograph courtesy of Middleton Evans)

Baltimore County Memories . . .

"Essex is an English name meaning the 'east section'…it was once a colonial estate called Paradise Farm. In 1909, the farm was sold off in lots by the Taylor Land Company and the first house was built in what is now Essex."

- Elaine Bunting and Patricia D'Amario, *Counties of North Maryland*

"The Home Interest Club's earliest members were farm women who spent all day with their chores…My grandmother would feed ten to fifteen farmhands for dinner in the middle of the day and everything they ate came from the farm."

- Bobbie Hudson, Sparks, third generation Club Member

"My father always had a beautiful garden [in Sparrows Point] in the backyard of the house. He never sold his vegetables, just shared them with neighbors."

- Annie Ruth Randolph, Interviewed by Louis S, Diggs, *From the Meadows to the Point*

"In 1878, the Baltimore County Grange held a small one-day agricultural fair…The Agricultural Society of Baltimore County was established to organize the Maryland State Fair [the next year]."

- Elaine Bunting and Patricia D'Amario, *Counties of North Maryland*

"I was born 77 years ago on Warren Road, Cockeysville and then moved to York Road between Padonia and Texas Roads across from my Grandfather's, William G. Parks, farm. My Uncle Douglas Parks lived above the farm next to the Almshouse. The cemetery is where we bailed hay and picked blackberries down by the stream. As kids, we use to go swimming in the pond behind the Almshouse. We had to walk through a pig's pen to get there."

- Ruth Ann Lee Roberts, Cockeysville

"My father's family, The Bishops, owned a 152-acre farm in Cockeysville. The farm raised goldfish that were sold nationwide and in Europe. The Bishops also furnished the goldfish for the ponds at the old Towson Courthouse. Hayfields Farm was nearby and Wallis Warfield (later the Duchess of Windsor) would visit her Merryman side of the family there. Daddy and Wallis were teenage friends. Wallis loved to sit on the hood of my father's car as he drove under the old Cockeysville Underpass and tooted the horn."

- Jeanne Fagan, Cockeysville

"My mother, my grandparents, my great grandparents and myself grew up in Baltimore County and it is our heritage. We all grew up in the 'Hereford Zone' on Big Falls Road which is now a part of a legacy. It is a small enclave of African American Families that worked, lived and loved Hereford and Baltimore County."

- April N. Goldring, Hereford

"I remember life on the farm in Baltimore County. Fields with mules and work horses instead of show horses. Potash for fertilizer came from burning over the fields in the spring, before plowing. Dairy farmers carried their milk in cans to the 'milk stand' on the main road to be picked up and taken to the dairy. The cans were returned the next day. Corn was cut by hand and put in shocks in the field. Cornfields seemed dotted with 'tepees'."

- Helen Mayo, Glencoe

"We remember the cows at the farm of Dr. Gorsuch on York Road in Timonium. During the early 1950s, it was near the corner of Crowther Avenue and York Road. There were only five streets in the heart of Timonium. All the adults knew us, so we had to have good behavior."

- Victoria Gerber Powell and Joyce Mather Pickett, Timonium

"My family moved from Canton to Dundalk for a better neighborhood experience in 1959. However, we traded the 'black soot' from Standard Oil to the 'red dust' of Sparrows Point. Of course, that was good because it was a sign that Bethlehem Steel was producing steel."

- Buzz Chriest, Dundalk

"When I came to Towson in 1962, the town was still much as it had been since World War II. I used to hear cows from the Sheppard Pratt herd lowing as they pastured where the Versailles Apartments are."

- Richard Parsons, West Towson

"Boordy Vineyard on Long Green Pike in Hydes was once a farm owned by Thomas Gittings...It was originally called 'Gittings Choice'...and tobacco was grown there before the Revolutionary War."

- Elaine Bunting and Patricia D'Amario, *Counties of North Maryland*

"The average Baltimore County farm is ninety-one acres. Most agricultural facilities are family-owned and operated... including many of the nurseries and greenhouses in the County."

- Office of Communications, Baltimore County Government

"The land we will preserve...will go a long way toward protecting the environment and sustaining the County's $300,000,000 agriculture industry."

- Jim Smith, Baltimore County Executive

"The Baltimore County Center for Maryland Agriculture is being developed on a 149-acre property... located on the corner of Shawan and Cuba Roads. The center will consolidate many of the support services for the agricultural community, promote the future sustainability of the agricultural industry, serve as an educational resource center and field destination for school children and adults, and provide open space benefits of walking and equestrian trail riding."

- Environmental Protection & Resource Management, Baltimore County Government

"Many horse shows have taken place over the years. One of the most unusual was the Piney Hill Jockey Club Horse Show, started in 1943 by northern Baltimore County residents, to support their love of horses. Dr. Dick Gorsuch, a local veterinarian of the day, would proudly ride his white mule to the Piney Hill Show to demonstrate that the love for animals did not stop with horses. The Greenspring Hounds Pony Club thrived for years, teaching the next generation of riders how to mount, clean, tack, and groom their ponies and the Mt. Carmel Hounds is just one of the fox hunts that crosses farmer's fields in Baltimore County. Today, Baltimore County retains its love of the horse, and many equestrian events occur throughout the year. Breeding and training farms may feel the pressure of urban sprawl, but they determinedly continue the time-honored traditions connecting horse and man. And today, more than one local teenager has a dream to join the U.S. Equestrian Team at the next Olympic Games."

- Janey Mowell, Glencoe

Chapter 6

COMMERCE & INDUSTRY

*W*hile farming produced the most important commodities during the first two centuries of Baltimore County's existence, the development of commerce and industry associated with agriculture formed an integrated relationship that created a broad economic base.

What powered the vast portion of the economy in the eighteenth and nineteenth centuries was water; water which powered mills. The availability of water and the creation of millraces provided the necessary energy in an era before steam, gas and electricity. Accordingly, mill towns grew around the mills which produced flour, textiles, paper and even gunpowder. Sawmills also cut wood for a variety of construction projects. It is estimated that over one hundred mills of varying types existed throughout the County during this era.

In addition to mills, limekilns produced the lime needed to improve agricultural productivity while quarrying for marble and granite were significant enterprises during the first half of Baltimore County's history. Mining for copper and chrome were also major industries before the Civil War but paled in comparison to the production of iron ore and pig iron. While these industrial activities have faded in importance and the primitive furnaces, kilns and mines have fallen silent, the names of places and streets still reflect this heritage.

As the industrial revolution took hold in the latter portion of the 1700s and progressed through the next century, the transition from rural gristmills, textile mills and diminutive iron furnaces gave way to industrial plants with steam power and technology like the Bessemer process. Thus, the formation of industries such as Bethlehem Steel, Black & Decker and Harry T. Campbell Sons' Corporation became the forces which drove the economy. Along with steel and shipbuilding, the production of airplanes at the Glenn L. Martin plant provided a formidable industrial capacity. Even breweries and distilling companies came to reside within the confines of the County; thus, demonstrating the business and commercial range of this municipality.

Built on 350 years of economic growth, Baltimore County is currently the home to an estimated 22,000 retail, industrial and wholesale businesses. With the assistance of Baltimore County, commercial partnerships, retail malls, corporate campuses, federal headquarters, factories and technological facilities abound. The County is a microcosm of our national economy.

"Profit is not the legitimate purpose of business. The legitimate purpose of business is to provide a product or service that people need and do it so well that it's profitable."

James Rouse

The Green Spring Valley Branch of the Baltimore and Susquehanna Railroad, which crossed the Falls Road Turnpike, was constructed in 1832. It was the second pioneering railroad out of Baltimore. In the same year, the Valley Inn, previously the Brooklandville House, was built. It has served as a tavern, housed the post office, was an Abercrombie and Fitch sporting goods store during Prohibition and is now a popular restaurant. (Photograph courtesy of John McGrain and the Historical Society of Baltimore County)

An early nineteenth century drawing of Ellicott's Iron Works, known officially as the "Patapsco Rolling and Slitting Mills and Nail Manufactory of Ellicott & Co." The factory was located on the Patapsco River, downstream from the mills at Oella and just upstream of the present day Ellicott City Bridge. The site was later occupied by the Granite Manufactory, a cotton mill, and was eventually destroyed by the great flood of July 1868. (Drawing courtesy of the Baltimore County Public Library)

Wilson's Lumber Yard, like so many other lumber yards in Baltimore County, started in business before the twentieth century as a result of the growth of communities like Catonsville. *Note that coal was sold by the ton or by an entire car load. (Photograph courtesy of the Catonsville Room, Baltimore County Public Library)

J.G. Owens and Company was a combination hardware and general store which served the town of Catonsville, circa 1890. The building also leased space to the Odd Fellows Lodge on the second floor. (Photograph courtesy of the Catonsville Room, Baltimore County Public Library)

Two Towson businesses were housed in this building occupying 414 York Road. In the late 1890s, both shoes and tobacco were considered necessities for most men. As time progressed, the building was used as the Country Coffee Shop and then as a restaurant known as the "Real Thing." (Photograph courtesy of the Baltimore County Public Library)

Ore and other raw materials were still being brought to Sparrows Point on sailing ships in the early 1900s. (Photograph courtesy of the Dundalk-Patapsco Neck Historical Society)

The combination of steam and steel were major components of the Baltimore County economy as shown in this 1900s photograph of the Sparrows Point blast furnaces and the railroad tracks on Third Street. (Photograph courtesy of the Dundalk-Patapsco Neck Historical Society)

Built in 1847, the Phoenix Textile Mill was the last of its type in Baltimore County. In general, textile mills employed over 2000 workers, more than any other type of industry in Baltimore County. Sixty percent of the workers were women. This photograph was taken during the early 1920s. (Photograph courtesy of the Baltimore County Public Library)

Peter M. Dotterweich operated a barbershop at his home on Foster Avenue. At the time when the family moved into that area, it was part of a large German community located in Baltimore County. The wall calendar is dated 1913. Dotterweich always gave toys to the children when he cut their hair. (Photograph courtesy of Dr. Andrew Dotterweich)

This ice cream store stood at the southeast corner of Shawn and Fall Roads, circa 1920. For many children as well as adults, a cold ice cream cone was a real summer treat before electric refrigerators became common place. Like most stores at the time, they also sold a variety of other items, making them the forerunner to the modern convenience store. (Photograph courtesy of the Baltimore County Public Library)

In the 1920s, Halethorpe's business district was the center of town where trains, roads and trolley cars provided excellent transportation for commercial and private travel. This photograph was taken from Potomac Avenue looking across the Pennsylvania Railroad tracks, now Amtrak. The center of town had a post office, grocery store, hardware store, community hall and even a bowling alley. The Francis Avenue Bridge and Southwestern Boulevard were built on this site after World War II. Thus, Halethorpe lost its commercial center. (Photograph courtesy of the Halethorpe Heritage Committee)

Throughout the 1920s, Conrad Shanawolf (left) and Thomas Dail (right) operated this rolling store throughout the southeastern section of Baltimore County. In its day, it was considered a real convenience store as were the many hucksters who sold their wares on County streets. (Photograph courtesy of the Dundalk-Patapsco Neck Historical Society)

Many quality hotels existed along Washington Boulevard during the 1920 and 30s. However, the Baltimore Tourist Camp provided very modest accommodations for people on a limited budget who traveled along the highway. Washington Boulevard, Route 1, was the major highway along the east coast from colonial times until Route 95 was built. (Photograph courtesy of the Baltimore County Public Library)

Towson Theater opened on March 1, 1928 at a cost of $100,000 and was built on the site of the old Towson Hotel. The theater provided area residents with entertainment for decades. (Drawing courtesy of Special Collections, Albin O. Kuhn Library & Gallery, University of Maryland, Baltimore County)

During the 1930s, the Carney Bakery was located on Harford Road. The Bakery stayed in business during the Depression by delivering doughnuts at twenty cents a dozen, loaves of bread for ten cents and small pies for nineteen cents. (Photograph courtesy of the Greater Parkville Community Council History Committee)

A worker attends to pouring of pig iron at the Sparrows Point plant during the Depression. The process had not changed a great deal since its inception. (Photograph courtesy of the Dundalk-Patapsco Neck Historical Society)

The Dundalk Village Shopping Center, completed in 1919, became the center of the community. Shown in the 1930s, the stores were able to stay in business during the Depression. The shopping area now has the "Main Street Maryland" historical designation. (Photograph courtesy of the Dundalk-Patapsco Neck Historical Society)

The Stebbins-Anderson coal and wood business was located on York Road in Towson. Seen in 1937, the company displayed their fleet of trucks. As heating fuels changed, so did the products that Stebbins-Anderson sold. As with any good business, they stayed in tune with market trends for several decades. (Photograph courtesy of the Catonsville Room, Baltimore County Public Library)

A Boeing 314 flying boat made a landing in front of the Pan American Airways terminal building. Flying boats were considered to be the future of aviation and Baltimore County was at the cutting edge of this technology. However, practicality and World War II made this type of commercial aviation obsolete. The field for land-based planes, behind the hanger, was not completed until 1941 and was called Harbor Field. (Photograph courtesy of the Dundalk-Patapsco Neck Historical Society)

The Milton Inn, on York Road in Sparks, set an elaborate table in the early 1940s. Popular for decades, many long-term residents have enjoyed special occasions at this landmark establishment. (Photograph courtesy of the Baltimore County Public Library)

The SS Patrick Henry was the first of more than 2700 Liberty ships to be built at Bethlehem Steel Company's Fairfield Shipyard. The SS Patrick Henry was being launched while fireboats sent up a shower of water in celebration of the event. (Photograph courtesy of the Baltimore County Public Library)

The Company Store in Sparrows Point was a main center of retail commerce for steel workers and their families, circa the 1940s. (Photograph courtesy of the Dundalk-Patapsco Neck Historical Society)

After rationing meat, sugar and other basic commodities, during World War II, the site of full shelves at the grocery market was certainly welcome. The sales people were ready for business as the Washington Grocery Store prepared for its grand opening in 1946. The store was located at the corner of Winters Lane and Edmondson Avenue in the African American section of Catonsville. (Photograph courtesy of Louis Diggs)

Industrial activity, along with the accompanying pollution, was apparent at Sparrows Point in 1954. In that era, smoke was still considered a sign of prosperity. (Photograph courtesy of the Dundalk-Patapsco Neck Historical Society)

"We'll see ya at the Circle" was a phrase understood by most Dundalk and Sparrows Point residents in the 1950s. The Circle, located at Dundalk Avenue and Gusryan Street, was a popular place to gather on the weekends for a cube steak sandwich, fries and a shake. Teenagers would eat in their cars and enjoy hanging-out on the large parking lot. In its last iteration, the restaurant was called the Circle Drive-In Ice Cream Co. (Photograph courtesy of the Dundalk-Patapsco Neck Historical Society)

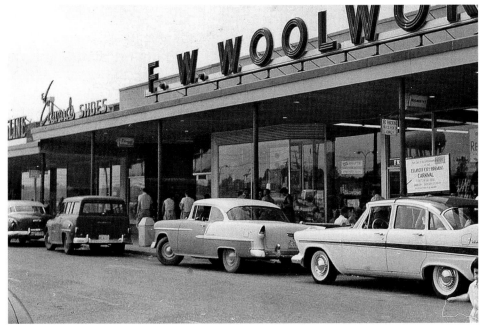

In 1958, Woolworth's was a popular chain of stores in the Baltimore area. This store was located in the Ingelside Shopping Center on Baltimore National Pike. The Ingleside and Westview Shopping centers were strip malls located next to each other which provided suburban shopping for the southwestern section of Baltimore County. (Photograph courtesy of the Historical Society of Baltimore County)

Before national chains dominated the market, drugstores like Reads provided a neighborly approach to the medical needs of the community. The local chain had stores all over the Baltimore area and popularized the slogan "Run Right to Reads." This Reads, shown circa the 1950s, was located in the Dundalk Village Shopping Center on Shipping Place. (Photograph courtesy of the Dundalk-Patapsco Neck Historical Society)

Diners became popular all over Baltimore in the 1950s and 60s. The Towson Diner on York Road was owned by the Stratakis family when this photograph was taken in 1960. In 1998, the diner was demolished and replaced by a larger establishment. Similar diners, clad in chrome panels, such as the Double T Dinner on Rolling Road and Route 40 are similar in design and just as popular. (Photograph courtesy of the Baltimore County Public Library)

Providing quality clothing for its clients, the Hutzler's Department Store in Eastpoint Mall, as well as other suburban locations, provided a grand shopping experience in the 1960s. Baltimore County malls were a welcome departure from the trip downtown to Howard Street. (Photograph courtesy of the Baltimore County Public Library)

The WFBR Radio Station's traffic helicopter surveyed the condition of the Beltway in Lansdowne by the Carling Brewery in 1964. For years, the Brewery, a local landmark, was considered a state-of-the-art plant. It even had a brewing tank displayed in its front window. (Photograph courtesy of the Baltimore County Public Library)

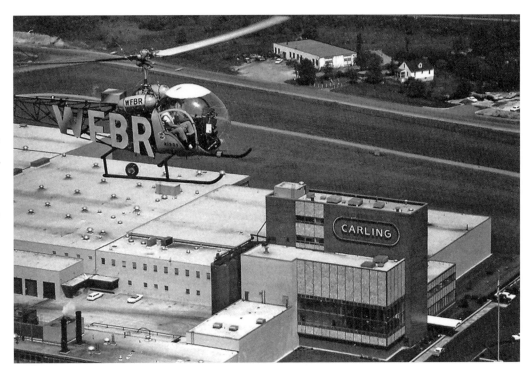

Located at Fifth and Brentwood Avenues in Dundalk, the Brentwood Inn was a locally celebrated gathering place. Noted for its wine cellar, the Brentwood Inn had these postcards printed to promote the business in the 1960s. (Postcard courtesy of the Baltimore County Public Library)

The streetscape of York Road in the center of Towson looked dramatically less crowded in 1967 than it does today. The buildings in the center foreground had to be demolished to make way for the Towson Roundabout. (Photograph courtesy of Jacques Kelly)

For decades, Windy Valley Farms was an unpretentious ice cream stop for children and families, as seen in 1979. The store was adjacent to Greenspring Station at West Joppa Road in Brooklandville. (Photograph courtesy of the Baltimore County Public Library)

The Stoneleigh Shopping Center, located at the corner of York Road and Regester Avenue, was designed by Oliver Stone. This photograph shows that this attractive piece of commercial real estate still looks the same as it did in 1982. (Photograph courtesy of the Baltimore County Public Library)

In 1986, a ribbon cutting ceremony marked the first ATM in Baltimore County. The Sparks Bank was the first financial institution to take advantage of this technology. At the time, this was a noteworthy financial event which would ultimately change the way people would conduct their banking. (Photograph courtesy of Historical Society of Baltimore County)

The Country Fair Inn occupied the large brick home once owned by Samuel Owings on Painters Mill Road. Kathy White, pastry chef, and Michel Haudebert, chef, proudly presented an artistic desert in 1987. Despite public protest, the popular restaurant was later demolished and replaced by a high rise building. (Photograph courtesy of the Baltimore County Public Library)

The Little Tavern restaurants were quite small but their unique design made them one of the most recognizable establishments in the Baltimore area. This Little Tavern, shown in 1988 on York Road, is now only a memory. (Photograph courtesy of the Baltimore County Public Library)

Friendly Farms in Upperco, was started by Dot Wihelm and her husband in the 1950s. It quickly became known for its Maryland crab cakes. The duck pond seemed to be as popular as the food. (Photograph courtesy of the Baltimore County Public Library)

For special occasions, the Green Spring Inn was one of several restaurants throughout Baltimore County that provided an elegant dining experience. Many fond memories were shared over a meal at this establishment. After fifty three years, the Green Spring Inn closed its doors in the fall of 1989. (Photograph courtesy of the Baltimore County Public Library)

"Town Gone" was written on the reverse side of this 2001 photograph and describes the physical, psychological and economic impact of the decline of steel production in the Baltimore area and the nation in general. (Photograph courtesy of the Dundalk-Patapsco Neck Historical Society)

As part of Baltimore County's Renaissance Redevelopment Program, the County initiated an Urban Design Assistance Team program for Randallstown in 2003. The effort drew hundreds of residents into a collaborative process that included strong recommendations for a multi-faceted community center. The County broke ground on the 58,000-square-foot center, the largest ever to be built in the County, in the fall of 2007. (Photograph courtesy of the Baltimore County Office of Communications)

The revitalization of Hunt Valley Towne Centre transformed a decaying mall into an upscale shopping and dining attraction. The Towne Centre replicated the retail success of The Avenue at White Marsh. (Photograph courtesy of the Baltimore County Office of Communications)

Baltimore County Memories . . .

"The most dramatic change to come out of this revolutionary era was the rise of Baltimore. With commerce flowing through its port and merchants uniting their energies, the town grew into a city that gave direction to the rest of the county until the city-county split in the 1850s."

- Neal A. Brooks, Eric G. Rokel and William C. Hughs, *A History of Baltimore County*

"In 1929, [Black and Decker] outfitted a Travel-Air monoplane as a flying showroom for products useful in reconditioning aircraft engines."

- H. George Hahn and Carl Behm III, *Towson: A Pictorial History of a Maryland Town*

"Temple M. Joyce, a Baltimore Polytechnic Institute (Poly) graduate and Lehigh University aeronautical engineering graduate, was inspired by the Baltimore Aero Meet [Halethorpe], 1910...after World War I, he formed the Berliner-Joyce Aircraft Company in Dundalk. The company eventually moved to California and later became North American Rockwell."

- Lewis Porter, Towson

"Martin's had a bowling league, roller skating, circuses and a tumbling team. People were happy and stayed in the area."

- Ray and Marge Barhight, *Middle River Oral History Project*

"During World War II, some of the women became very good welders, especially on intricate parts and where it demanded a more delicate touch...We had women who sorted rivets. Could you think of a more dull job in the whole world! I think 95% of the women that were hired worked out very well and they were very proud of the job they did."

- Charles Bader, *Middle River Oral History Project*

"There was a big laundry up in Essex [during WWII]. The boys in the boarding houses would do their wash and bring it back and hang it outside."

- Ed and Emma Blazek, Middle River Oral History Project

"Victory Villa Drug Store was our hangout...they had the booze and that's all the young people wanted to think of. My girlfriend and I used to go to the Hiway Theater and the bowling alley."

- Julie Kauffman, Middle River Oral History Project

"In the Aero Acres shopping center [during the 1940s], there was a restaurant called the Bomber on the corner, behind the sewing factory...that is all torn down now."

- Linda and Roger Magsamen, Middle River Oral History Project

"As a youngster, a Sunday excursion consisted of a long drive through the scenic pastures of Greenspring Valley and a stop for homemade ice cream at Meadowbrook Farms. Since then, I've witnessed many changes in our County. The 1940s expansion of the war industry brought Bendix in Towson, Glenn L. Martin's in Essex and Bethlehem Steel in Dundalk, which fostered a huge influx of people to the County. Small towns like Towson, Essex and Cockeysville burgeoned into major commercial centers. With the growth came losses of old institutions

and a simpler time, which can still be somewhat captured in visits to Ellicott City and Hereford. In spite of the sadness of loss and the excitement of new tomorrows, what remains constant is the diversity of the citizens and the commitment to preserve the best of yesterday while embracing the future."

- Reverend Rodney Gatzke, Towson

"I will always remember going to Price's Dairy, getting my hair cut at Pete's Barbershop (he would always include a little kid's shave), walking to the drugstore for candy and feeling rich if some relative gave us a dollar."

- David Gaine, Gwynn Oak

"I remember walking over to a small store in Mount Washington to buy baseball cards each spring and summer. I think it was a nickel a pack, and it included six to eight cards and gum. We would often 'flip' the cards at recess up against a wall. Whoever 'topped' the baseball card first would win all the cards that had been flipped...In the early 1960s, my brother and I were very enterprising and would go around the neighborhood taking our neighbors' trash out to the road weekly. We were paid a quarter per family. In the winter, we shoveled their sidewalks when it snowed for a dollar."

- Jim Wharton, Mount Washington

"We had 'arabbers' with their horse-drawn carts bringing delicious strawberries and soft crabs in the summer. There was nothing like a soft-crab sandwich on a Saturday afternoon, with a slice of tomato from the garden of our neighbor, Mr. Joe."

- Nancy Eubert, Parkville, Carney and Cub Hill

"Baltimore County's industries have contributed ships and aircraft, scientific instruments, agricultural products, tools and metals to the national needs. Its quarries, forests and streams have been indispensable resources, freely shared."

- J. Millard Tawes, Governor of Maryland, 1959-1967

"I started working for Eddie's Grocery Store in 1951 and bought the establishment in 1983. My wife and I changed the name to The Store and developed loyal customers through personal services such as home delivery. The Store supported Christmas tree sales by the Lions Club and assisted with food baskets for community members in need."

- Frank and Mary Ellen Evans, Catonsville

"I started traveling to the Circle after dances around 1974. You could find almost anyone at the Circle. The owner and his wife worked every night, and they had one cook in the kitchen. If you had a hot car, the Circle was the place to be."

- Cathy Bevins, Dundalk

"A joy for all of us was Sunday dinner at Bernie Lee's old Penn Hotel or a chicken pot pie for lunch in the Valley Room of the sadly gone Hutzler's."

- Richard Parsons, West Towson

"While the County was primarily agrarian during the 1800s, the County ultimately became an industrial center, many of its factories being the first in the country. Villages grew up around these factories; the factories have long been closed but the villages remain. The reduction in industry has been replaced by technology and today Baltimore County is a leader in technology. It is a survivor!"

- T. Bryan McIntire, Baltimore County Councilman, 3rd District

350

YEARS

BALTIMORE
COUNTY
MARYLAND

1659 - 2009

Chapter 7

LABOR

*T*he agricultural, commercial and industrial prowess of Baltimore County has been well documented and stands as a source of economic pride. However, without a workforce comprised of energetic men and women, this rich legacy would not have transpired.

As delineated in previous chapters, the production of agricultural products created a massive demand for all forms of labor. Most of this labor involved backbreaking toil from sun-up to sun-down. Ore production, quarrying, milling and an expanding industrial capacity also required a prodigious workforce. Fortunately, with the assistance of immigration and natural population growth, labor kept pace. Males and females often worked along with children in the fields as well as the factories. Accordingly, free and slave labor powered the pre-Civil War economy and Baltimore County mirrored the national controversy over the issues of slavery, servitude and exploitation.

The rise of industrialization in Baltimore County provided a plethora of jobs before the twentieth century, while World War I only fueled a growing demand for labor. Generally speaking, this prosperity for employees continued during the "Roaring 20s." However, the Great Depression that followed had devastating effects on industries like Bethlehem Steel causing nineteen percent unemployment in the County during 1931. Only with President Franklin Roosevelt's New Deal programs and the outbreak of war in Europe did the economy begin to improve.

With the beginning of World War II, the need for labor once again dramatically increased. For instance, Glenn L. Martin's employment rose from 4,100 workers in 1939 to 53,000 in 1942. To fill this staggering capacity, laborers came to the region from the around the United States for employment. At the conclusion of the war, Baltimore County's population had increased by sixty-six percent.

Since World War II, Baltimore County's employment history has continued in an impressive manner due to the successful transition from industrial-based jobs to service-based employment. The age of technology has also created opportunities for a new generation of computer literate individuals. Of the 411,000 people employed over the age of sixteen, twenty five percent now work in occupations related to education, health and human services. Another ten percent work in retail jobs while less than one percent is employed in a field associated with agriculture. While strikes and labor disputes with business owners have occurred for generations and some have been less than productive, the interplay between these two economic forces has ultimately forged a prosperous region. Thus opportunity, even in challenging times, remains a part of the Baltimore County legacy in the twenty-first century.

"The true way to render ourselves happy is to love our work and find in it our pleasure."

Francoise De Motteville

Limestone burning began in Texas in 1804, with no less than thirty-seven kilns in operation by 1852. When wages were reduced from $1.50 to $1.25 per day in 1866, 250 workers, many of them Irish immigrants, went on strike in an aggressive demand for higher pay. However, the violent and non-violent actions of the strikers were not highly successful. The limekilns pictured here, have been proposed as a site for an archaeological and restoration project in Texas. (Photograph courtesy of the Baltimore County Public Library)

Employees and their families gathered in front of the Ashland Iron Works, circa 1870. While the pay was generally low, the hours were long and the work was grueling, jobs in the pig iron industry were still available in this era. The next two decades, however, proved more difficult as a result of competition from the new Pennsylvania Steel Company at Sparrows Point in 1887 and following a major depression in 1893. Ultimately, Ashland Iron closed because it became an obsolete facility that was no longer profitable. As a result, many of its workers migrated to Sparrows Point for their livelihood. (Photograph courtesy of the Baltimore County Public Library)

Tilly Mathews, is seen on the grounds of Hillside Farm in Warren, circa 1892. She traveled with the Baldwin family, along with several other servants, from the North Charles Street residence to Warren each summer. Tilly was the daughter of "Aunt Hester," who had been a slave before the Civil War. (Photograph courtesy of the Trustees of the Bunker Hill Foundation)

A gigantic open hearth ladle discharged a stream of molten steel into one of a row of molds at the Sparrows Point plant. A workman at the right, tended to the bottom pour method of filling the molds. In the 1890s, this was a physically demanding and dangerous job, especially during the summer months. (Photograph courtesy of the Baltimore County Public Library)

Paid for every 100 bricks loaded, an African American worker transported bricks from the kiln to the loading dock at the Burns and Russell Brickyard in the early 1900s. The bricks were then transported to sailing ships and traveled from Dundalk to the harbor in Baltimore. This process became even more important after the Baltimore Fire of 1904 caused a demand for building supplies. (Photograph courtesy of the Dundalk-Patapsco Neck Historical Society)

At Spring Grove Mental Hospital, some labor was both productive and therapeutic. In 1899, the basket making shop was one such example. (Photograph courtesy of the Catonsville Room, Baltimore County Public Library)

Without the use of a crane, it took John Henry Wagner, a team of ten men and two boys, to move an immense boiler which was being drawn along Taylor Avenue, circa 1900. Wagner was one of the owners of Wagner & Chenoweth of Parkville. (Photograph courtesy of the Baltimore County Public Library)

117

Albert M Weis' store on York Road sold all types of goods. As was typical of the era, circa 1914, small shops required the labor of the entire family. (Photograph courtesy of the Baltimore County Public Library)

Two women work the lathes at the original Black & Decker factory in 1918. The pot-belled stove was the only source of heat in the winter. Black & Decker prospered during World War I and grew to become a major industrial corporation, hiring hundreds of workers in the Baltimore area. (Photograph courtesy of the Baltimore County Public Library)

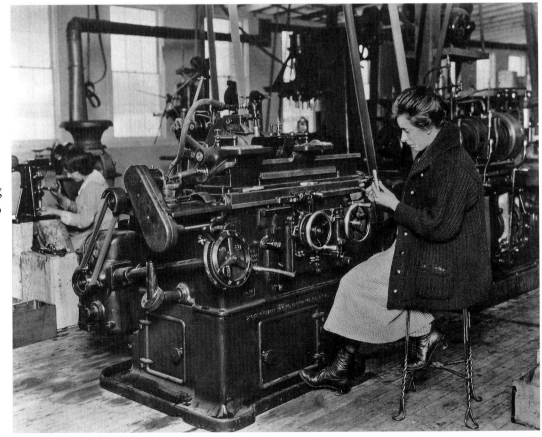

While water in plastic bottles is the current trend, these workers in 1926 operated glass bottle-capping machinery at the Caton Spring Water Company. The glass bottles were then placed in wooden crates for shipping. (Photograph courtesy of the Baltimore County Public Library)

In 1938, 200 women per shift worked at the Sparrows Point mill sorting room where each sheet of tin was examined for defects. The women became known as "Tin Floppers." (Photograph courtesy of the Dundalk-Patapsco Neck Historical Society)

During World War II, the women working in factories, who replaced men that left to go to war, became known as "Rosie the Riveters" even if they did not actually perform that specific task. These "Rosies" worked on the nose of a Martin XPB-2M-Mars seaplane in 1941. The accomplishments of Baltimore women during the war were legendary. (Photograph courtesy of the Baltimore County Public Library)

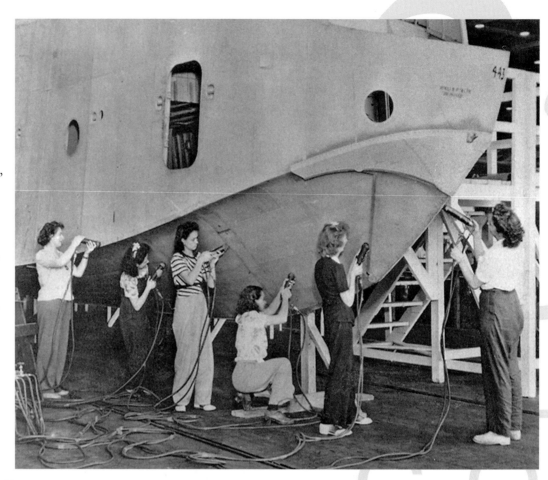

Assembly line work was a tedious job during World War II. However, the women who operated the armature coil winders at the Towson Black & Decker plant in 1945 were proud to contribute to the war effort. Many of the women, who filled in for the men in the military, often worked double shifts. (Photograph courtesy of the Baltimore County Public Library)

Quitting time at Sparrows Point involved a race for the "Red Rocket," proving that mass transit was still a necessity after World War II. (Photograph courtesy of the Dundalk-Patapsco Neck Historical Society)

In 1958, Elmer Schmidt ran one of the last blacksmiths' shops in Baltimore County. The George H. Schmidt Blacksmith Shop was located on Long Green Pike and Manor Road. (Photograph courtesy of the Baltimore County Public Library)

Cashiers lined up at a Ben Franklin store in the 500 Block of Eastern Avenue in Essex. Shortly after this photograph was taken in early 1957, a fire destroyed the entire block of buildings in August of 1957. (Photograph courtesy of the Baltimore County Public Library)

Joshua Cockey and waiters at the Limestone Dinner Theater seemed to be having as much fun as the patrons in 1960. Cockey and his wife founded and managed the dinner theater. (Photograph courtesy of the Baltimore County Public Library)

Harry Herman was photographed working on his eightieth birthday at Herman's Bakery on Holabird Avenue. Herman's Bakery was considered a local institution in the community. (Photograph courtesy of the Dundalk-Patapsco Neck Historical Society)

Throughout Baltimore County's history, the production of cotton duck has been a major part of the economy. D. H. Halton and Charles Brown cut bolts of cotton duck for shipment at the Alberton - Daniels Textile Mill in 1967. (Photograph courtesy of Jacques Kelly)

The County Restaurant on York Road was a fixture in Towson for decades. Before it closed in the 1990s, owner John Karsos is seen with Mary, a member of the staff for over twenty years. (Photograph courtesy of the Baltimore County Public Library)

While large grocery store chains provide a majority of the food for Baltimore County residents, local entrepreneurs still sell produce in much the same way as their ancestors did, especially during the summer months. (Photograph courtesy of the Baltimore County Office of Communications)

The traditions of hard work and a sense of responsibility are carried on by these contemporary steel workers. (Photograph © 2002, courtesy of Jay Mallin)

Road and sidewalk repair is a physically demanding job. Crews of Baltimore County workers are kept busy with the never-ending task of maintaining the County's 2600 miles of roads and more than 400 bridges. However, it is a service that is appreciated by all County residents. (Photograph courtesy of the Baltimore County Office of Communications.)

During the economic recession of 2008, a man out of work was forced by desperation to sell roses on Perring Parkway near Carney. (Photograph courtesy of Bill Barry, Director of Labor Studies on the CCBC Dundalk campus)

As service work becomes a more prominent part of the Baltimore County economy, jobs in the fast food industry are increasingly important to young people looking for employment. Such jobs provide training and skills for individuals entering the work force. (Photograph courtesy of Bill Barry, Director of Labor Studies on the CCBC Dundalk campus)

Baltimore County Memories . . .

"The newspapers were weak in reporting labor disputes, seldom quoting the arguments presented by the working people. The demands made by cotton spinners and miners were probably considered affronts to the established order, as audacious as Oliver Twist's request for more porridge in the almshouse refectory."

- John McGrain, *From Pig Iron to Cotton Duck: A History of Manufacturing in Baltimore County*

"In 1910…convicts labored on Liberty, Belair and Philadelphia Roads."

- Neal A. Brooks, Eric G. Rokel and William C. Hughs, *A History of Baltimore County*

"Since Maryland had no child labor laws until 1873, children as well as adults worked long hours in the mills for very little wages."

- Elaine Bunting and Patricia D'Amario, *Counties of North Maryland*

"If they didn't make the riveters…the early Rosies may have made the drills during the World War I effort."

- H. George Hahn and Carl Behm III, *Towson: A Pictorial History of a Maryland Town*

My grandfather, Albert Meyers, worked on the Baltimore and Ohio Railroad for years…He taught us the value of working hard.

- April N. Goldring, Hereford

"My father was born here in 1867 and my mother in 1877. There was a common bond. They knew that this was a war effort and everybody pitched in and forgot their differences if there were any."

- James Myers, Middle River Oral History Project

"I remember Mr. Staab…he was a paperhanger and a barber. My father would take me for haircuts there. He was located at Carroll Island Road and Eastern Avenue. His home later became a bar."

- Roay Ann McNamara, Seneca Creek / Middle River

"I thought Bethlehem Steel was a great place to work for a couple of reasons. During World War II, I remember my dad worked there and he was working seven days a week, twelve hours a day…I worked there starting in summer 1953, retired in 1996 and my son still works there. That was normal, many generations worked at Bethlehem Steel."

- Ed Bartee, Sr., Sparrows Point/Turner Station

"I remember our life in Dundalk being dominated by 'The Point.' North Point Boulevard would be solid with traffic headed to the steel mills and home from the steel mills two or three shifts a day. Most of my friends had fathers employed at the 'The Point.' Many nights the sky would be reddened by the glow of molten steel being poured. But all of that is gone now."

- Jean Bennett, Dundalk

"We had chores, as kids on our farm, but they were done early so we could go out and play."

- Donna Ensor Reihl, Parkville

"I remember the milkman from Wills Dairy delivering milk, plus eggs, butter, cream, bakery items, cottage cheese and the like. We also had an ice man come around and deliver our ice. I think his name was Mr. Potts."

- Roay Ann McNamara, Seneca Creek / Middle River

"Nancy Claster was 'Miss Nancy' in the show called 'Romper Room.' It aired all over the United States and in forty-five countries."

- Elaine Bunting and Patricia D'Amario, *Counties of North Maryland*

"A treat for my family would be to visit Pizza John's on Back River Neck Road in Essex. Pizza John's was known as the best place in town... and had only two rooms then. Everyone was nice while serving you. My favorite part of going inside to eat was watching through the glass window and seeing the people making the pizza. Now, Pizza John's is huge."

- Malina M. Colon, Essex

"It takes volunteer labor along with politicians, the schools and the Department of Recreation and Parks in order to provide sports and other programs for children. I have worked on behalf of the Arbutus community since 1948 to help organize after-school activities. No other work is as gratifying."

- George Kendrick, Arbutus

"I can walk into a local Dunkin Donuts and the woman behind the counter remembers who I am and what I usually order. I can take my car to a mechanic who worked on my dad's car... I meet people who bought their first car from my grandpa."

- Micah Kleid, Beth El Congregation of Baltimore

"My jobs included being a pin boy and getting paid five cents a game in 1937, ticket collector for the roller coaster at the Bay Shore Amusement Park at twenty-four cents an hour, selling crabs from the pier at Jones Creek...I have been volunteering at North Point State Park forever, and I am proud of the fact that I restored a 100-year-old fountain."

- Ranger Steve Tacos, Edgemere

"Just before she turned 100, my grandmother moved from her home in Timonium to an assisted living facility. She gave me an old rotting bench that she said had once been used by workers at the Warren mill. Thus began my fascination with the town—my grandmother's girlhood home—that was destroyed to make Loch Raven Reservoir. After she graduated from the eighth grade, my grandmother worked for a few months alongside her older sister in the mill's spinning room, transferring thread from spool to bobbin. She said the work wasn't hard, but it wasn't easy to stand on your feet for ten hours, either. When she died in 2006, at the age of 103, it was believed that she was the last surviving worker from Warren Manufacturing."

- Ann Eichler Kolakowski, Timonium

"Baltimore County has quickly become the County to work, live and to pursue the American Dream. I am pleased with the progress of Baltimore County for including opportunities for all citizens to be a part of this vision."

- Kenneth N. Oliver, Baltimore County Councilman, 4th District

350
YEARS
BALTIMORE
COUNTY
MARYLAND
1659 - 2009

Chapter 8

EDUCATION

COCKEYSVILLE ELEM
SCHOOL
GRADE 2
MISS YOUNG
MARYLAND
1956

*A*s Baltimore County began to grow and large land owners emerged, tutors were engaged to teach the children of the wealthy. As additional students were taken on from surrounding estates, informal schools for affluent families developed. Private institutions were also created under the direction of religious groups such as the Presbyterians and the Jesuits who focused their teachings on the Bible. While these early endeavors laid an educational foundation in the County, they consistently ignored the needs of most females, African Americans and the working class.

However, as early as 1723, the Maryland Assembly passed an Act to encourage public learning and to provide for the construction of one centrally located school in each county. Records support that such a school was indeed built in Baltimore County, but the exact location and details are uncertain.

It was not until one hundred and twenty five years later, in 1847, that the State Legislature mandated each political subdivision to create a system of free schools for all children. Consequently a Baltimore County Board of School Commissioners, later to be called the Board of Education, was appointed and a network of schools created. By 1900, despite changing state regulations, local politics and inconsistent fiscal support, the Baltimore County School System took shape with 191 schools serving 13,688 students.

Over the next several decades, Baltimore County Public Schools built new schools and became widely respected for its curriculum development. However, representative of society at large, education was still conducted in a segregated setting until the 1954 Supreme Court ruling required this social barrier to end. Five decades later, Baltimore County Public Schools reflected a highly diverse population of 107,300 students educated in 163 schools across the County.

Higher education in Baltimore County began its own legacy in the later part of the nineteenth century and has grown into a system that includes the University of Maryland, Baltimore County, Towson University, the Community Colleges of Baltimore County, Goucher College, Stevenson University and Loyola College. Like its K-12 counterparts, Baltimore County's colleges and universities have made an impact by providing higher education and skill training for the masses.

While Baltimore County still embraces a bifurcated tradition of private and public schools, one thing is certain. Education is provided in a spirit of equality with a goal of delivering the best twenty-first century instructional opportunities for all of its citizens.

"Education is the transmission of civilization."

Ariel and Will Durant

In 1855, Baltimore County designed a school house for "Homestead," Public School #4 in District 9. This design served as a model for one room schoolhouses throughout Baltimore County. This illustration was part of the 1855 School Board's Annual Report. (Drawing courtesy of the Baltimore County Public Library)

St. Timothy's Hall was incorporated in 1847 as a military school for young men. By 1850, the school had 132 students and 14 professors. However, the split between north and south during the Civil War closed the school. Later, a boarding school was opened. Today, a private school exists on the site. (Drawing courtesy of the Catonsville Room, Baltimore County Public Library)

It is thought that David F Painter, a teacher and photographer of school groups, took this photograph of his class. Taken only twenty-five years after the Civil War, segregated education would be the practice in the United States, in some states even after the Brown v. Board of Education case made "separate but equal" education unlawful in 1954. (Photograph courtesy of the Baltimore County Public Library)

Edmund W. Stabler, the Superintendent of The Manual Labor School for Indigent Boys in Catonsville, is seen in the woods with some of his students who had been gathering wild flowers, circa 1900. The school was established in 1839 and was inspired by a Quaker concept with the purpose of instructing and supporting indigent boys above the age of five years. UMBC currently occupies the site. (Photograph courtesy of the Baltimore County Public Library)

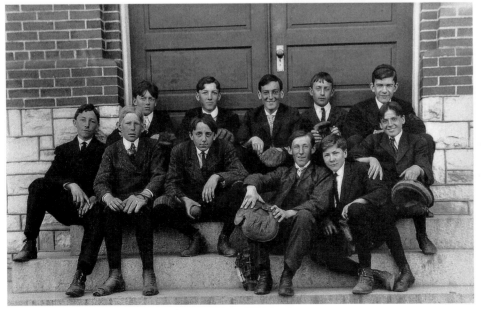

Sports have long been a Baltimore County tradition as evidenced by this 1908 Franklin High School baseball team. (Photograph courtesy of the Baltimore County Public Library)

A rare interior photograph of a classroom, circa 1910, gives a glimpse of what education was like almost a century ago. The school was Relay Elementary. (Photograph courtesy of the Catonsville Room, Baltimore County Public Schools)

A Towson High School home economics class received instruction on the proper techniques of mixing. In 1910, this procedure was done without the assistance of electrical appliances. *Note the instructions in chalk on the blackboard. (Photograph courtesy of the Baltimore County Public Library)

This building, which served as Towson High School, was built in 1907 on Allegheny Avenue. The two-story Italianate brick building, with its massive chimneys and open cupola, demonstrated the importance of education in the community. After becoming the headquarters for the Board of Education in 1925, it now continues in service, housing County agencies. (Photograph courtesy of John McGrain and the Historical Society of Baltimore County)

In 1915, McDonogh School students drill in formation while dressed in full cadet uniform. No doubt several of the students found their way to the front lines during World War I. (Photograph courtesy of the Baltimore County Public Library)

Oak Hill School #1 on the road from White Hall to Manor Road appeared to be the typical rural school in the 1920s. (Photograph courtesy of the Baltimore County Public Library)

To accommodate the increasing population as a result of industrial expansion, the new Sparrows Point High School was an impressive structure in 1921 and was one of the most modern educational facilities of its era. (Photograph courtesy of the Dundalk-Patapsco Neck Historical Society)

In 1921, Dundalk Elementary School was the only structure built in this section of town. However, residential and commercial development would soon follow. (Photograph courtesy of the Dundalk-Patapsco Neck Historical Society)

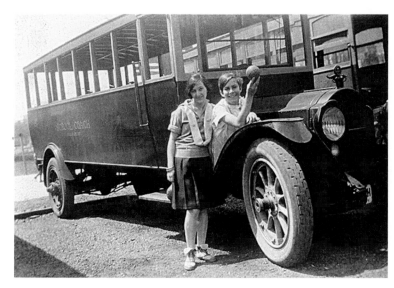

Elizabeth Klein Weimeister (right) is pictured here with high school friend Verena Carozza (left) in front of a school bus in September of 1928. Bus transportation was not free during that era and was a considerable expense for most families. Thus, many students walked or rode bikes to school. (Photograph courtesy of Elizabeth Klein Weimeister)

In 1951, when the new Franklin Elementary School was ready for occupancy, student labor was used to help move personal and school property. (Photograph courtesy of the Louise B. Goodwin Research Room, Reisterstown Branch, Baltimore County Public Library)

On a spring day in the late 1950s, the teachers at George Bragg School posed outside for a school portrait. (Photograph courtesy of the Baltimore County Public Library)

In 1954, on the eve of the Brown v. The Board of Education desegregation case, the African American staff of *The Eagle* worked on a newspaper at George Washington Carver High School on York Road in Towson. (Photograph courtesy of the Baltimore County Public Library)

Originally located in Baltimore City, Goucher College began its transition to Baltimore County in 1921. The construction of a new building, circa the 1950s, was observed by four curious students. In the early twenty-first century, Goucher found itself under construction once more. A new residence hall was completed in 2005 and the Athenaeum, a 100,000-square-foot, multipurpose facility featuring an expansive modern library, is expected to open in 2009. (Photograph courtesy of Goucher College)

The Lida Lee Tall Model School, on the grounds of Maryland State Teachers College, now Towson University, was built in 1960 and provided a progressive educational program for students while giving student teachers an opportunity to obtain valuable instructional experience. The school was demolished in April, 2007. (Photograph courtesy of the Baltimore County Public Library)

Like most elementary schools, this Cockeysville Elementary School class posed for a class picture in 1956. As the photograph suggests, class sizes grew large as Baltimore County's population expanded during the baby-boom era following WWII. (Photograph courtesy of the Historical Society of Baltimore County)

The station wagon provided by the Crosby School in Catonsville was a more personalized way to be transported to school than the traditional school bus provided by most institutions. More unique than the station wagon was the fact that four children in the photograph were the Henn Quadruplets. (Photograph courtesy of the Catonsville Room, Baltimore County Public Schools)

Dr. Thomas G. Pullen was principal of Catonsville High School, Superintendent of Baltimore County Public Schools and Superintendent of Schools for the State of Maryland. Well respected locally and nationally, Dr. Pullen was headed for a conference in London, circa the 1950s. (Photograph courtesy of the Catonsville Room, Baltimore County Public Schools)

Woodstock College was originally located along the Patapsco River in Woodstock and opened on September 22, 1869 as a Jesuit seminary; one of the oldest in the nation. The seminary stayed in operation until the decrease in candidates for the priesthood forced the institution to combine with a New York seminary in 1969. The original campus buildings in Woodstock, Maryland then transitioned into a Job Corps Center, while the campus grounds were made part of Patapsco Valley State Park. (Photograph courtesy of the Baltimore County Library)

Sister Mary Brenda Cherry and Sister Mary Stephana, Oblate Sisters of Providence, taught students at the Mount Providence Child Development Center located at the Mount Providence Convent in 1974. (Photograph courtesy of the Oblate Sister of Providence)

After graduating from Catonsville High School in 1942, Robert Y. Dubel served in the Marines during World War II. Once discharged, he earned several college degrees and became the Superintendent of Baltimore County Public Schools in 1976. After serving sixteen years as Superintendent, Dr. Dubel retired in 1992. (Photograph courtesy of Dr. Robert Y. Dubel)

Kindergarten students at Randallstown Elementary School participated in the "Body Rock" as part of a graduation day celebration in 1988. (Photograph courtesy of the Baltimore County Public Library)

For five decades, the Community College of Baltimore County (Essex Campus) has helped residents of all ages, backgrounds and interests earn college degrees, launch or expand careers and enrich their lives. (Photograph courtesy of the Community College of Baltimore County)

141

CCBC's state-of-the-art classrooms and laboratories enable Baltimore County's workforce to stay on the leading edge of developing technologies, shifts in work force demands and prepare for the emergence of a global community. (Photograph courtesy of the Community College of Baltimore County)

On a warm spring day, an informal learning experience reinforced classroom instruction on the Essex campus of the Community College of Baltimore County. (Photograph courtesy of the Community College of Baltimore County)

Kevin Clash was born in Turner Station where he put on shows for the children at his mother's day care. He has stated that "I was lucky enough to have been 'tossed' Elmo and the rest is history." (Photograph courtesy of Charla Helmers)

The Perry Hall High School band participated in the grand opening of the extension of Maryland Route 43 in Middle River on October 23, 2006. The band's performance not only provided experience for its members, it also provided a sense of community spirit. (Photograph courtesy of the Baltimore County Office of Communications)

In 2007, at the National Guard Armory in Towson, the Overlea High School Marine Corps JROTC participated in a Baltimore County celebration to commemorate Veterans Day. While all veterans were honored, the ceremony specifically focused on County employees who have served their country since September 11, 2001. (Photograph courtesy of the Baltimore County Office of Communications)

From its original roots as a normal school which trained teachers in the 1860s, Towson University has become a major institution of higher education in the Baltimore Metropolitan region with more than 18,000 students and 100 degree programs. The University currently combines training for teachers with research-based learning and practical applications delivered through internships and partnerships. (Photograph courtesy of Towson University)

The Albin O. Kuhn Library & Gallery serves as the architectural masterpiece as well as the academic center of the University of Maryland, Baltimore County campus. The 500 acre campus and most of the southwestern section of Baltimore County can be viewed from the seventh floor of this impressive structure which serves a diverse student body. (Photograph courtesy of Special Collections, Albin O. Kuhn Library & Gallery, University of Maryland, Baltimore County)

At Towson High School, like the other 162 County schools, welcome back ceremonies take place in late August of each year. School officials, teachers, as well as students anticipate the promise of a new school year. (Photograph courtesy of the Baltimore County Office of Communications)

Baltimore County Memories . . .

"In 1928, I entered the first grade. My mother used to drive me to school in a Model T Ford when Carroll Island Road was just a dirt road. The school had no running water...I recall carrying empty water buckets from the school to Mrs. Sticks' house on Bowleys Quarters Road. Each day two kids would be assigned water duty but we didn't mind; it was fun. Mr. Earle, the principal, would put a big dipper in the bucket and we all drank out of it."

- **Roay Ann McNamara, Seneca Creek / Middle River**

"As children, we attended Baltimore Highlands Elementary School, first through eleventh grade. I still am in contact with my fifth grade teacher...Our school held a May Fair every spring, complete with May Pole dance and the election of a King, Queen and Court."

- **Beatrice "Betty" Laukaitis Wassermann, Catonsville**

"I attended the same elementary and middle school as my mother. My parents met at the same high school I attended, Dulaney High School. My great-grandmother used to be principal of my elementary school, Timonium Elementary."

- **Jayme Schomann, Timonium**

"Towson Normal School provided me with the foundational skills to be successful in my teaching career. Even more important was the quest for learning that I developed so that I could improve my teaching proficiency through additional college work and ongoing connections with other professionals."

- **Nola Hale Zaiser Stuart, Towson Normal School, Class of 1929 Lutherville**

"In 1955, I was twelve years old, attending seventh grade at the Stemmers Run Junior High School Annex in Rosedale. Because of the overcrowding in public schools, the old Rosedale Elementary School building was where we went to school. Our school yard was too small to play baseball there."

- **Russ Sears, Rosedale**

"In 1941, Doc Minnegan coached all of the men's teams at the Maryland State Teachers College in Towson, now Towson University. In those days, we needed almost every male in the school to fill the team positions, especially soccer. The college had a British-made car that held six people and was used to transport team members to games in College Park, Pennsylvania, Frostburg and other venues. We had a great team."

- **John B. Shock, Jr., Athletic Hall of Fame, Towson State University Baldwin**

"In the 1940s participating in sports on a high school team was quite different than it is today! In my sophomore year, I was lucky enough to play for the junior varsity basketball team... As junior varsity team members, we had to use public transportation in order to get to some of our games. On the day of the game, we were excused from school quite early in order to get to the game on time. We walked to Towson and got on the #8 streetcar and then transferred once again. Getting to Dundalk and Sparrows Point was quite a challenge! We could hardly wait to make the varsity team!"

- **Jo Vitrano Miller, Towson High Class of 1949**

"My entire career in public education was in Baltimore County and spanned forty years. From a green little country girl starting out at Stemmers Run Junior High School in the fall of 1950, I eventually attained the position of Associate Superintendent of Instruction and held that position for fourteen years. Those were the golden years of curriculum development, when hundreds of teachers participated in summer workshops to write some of the most outstanding curriculum guides in the country. Our guides were purchased by school systems throughout the United States and by more than fifty foreign countries. Our instructional programs were defined by creativity, intelligence and caring. The emphasis was on the joy of teaching and of learning and on fundamental values in a democratic society."

- **Dr. Mary Ellen Saterlie, Associate Superintendent, Retired, Baltimore County Public Schools**

"When I retired as Superintendent of Schools in 1992, I was the longest serving Superintendent among the largest 25 school systems in the United States. I was often asked why and how I remained in that position for 16 years. My answer always was that I was invested in the system as a student and as an employee... From my student days, I remember superb teachers and strong discipline. In fact, once I had been exposed to the rigor of the faculty and curriculum at Catonsville High School, all of my undergraduate and graduate courses seemed quite easy.

It was an especially rewarding experience to serve as Superintendent in a school system where you grew up. I have rich memories of a Superintendency surrounded by outstanding teachers, administrators and supporting personnel. Baltimore County also had dedicated school boards. I have had a long love affair with the Baltimore County Public Schools."

- **Dr. Robert Y. Dubel, Superintendent, Retired Baltimore County Public Schools**

"To prepare students with a twenty-first-century education, the Baltimore County Public Schools has emphasized academic rigor for all students. The increasing diversity of the student population, the demand for achievement accountability at both the state and national levels and the variety of opportunities for learning are manifested in both program and structural changes... Since 1999, the system has been engaged in the largest school renovation and major maintenance program in the County's history, one that has impacted nearly every school.

- **Cliff Osborn, Coordinator of Social Studies, Retired, Baltimore County Public Schools**

"I am proud and humbled to lead Baltimore County Public Schools – the nation's 26th largest school system – into this new era where quality education for all children is mandated. During my tenure, our workforce and community have come to embrace what our children already know: that uniting to create boundless opportunity for all is much more important than any false barriers – race, disability, language, economics – that could keep us apart.... During this era of stringent accountability, our students are achieving at the highest levels of this school system's history. Historically, data has shown that increased diversity yields lower student performance. As our county has become more diverse, however, our school system, following its Blueprint for Progress, defies that correlation. Our school system today is recognized nationally and internationally for its innovative use of technology, talented school leadership, effective high schools, world-class fine arts instruction, and exemplary teachers. All of these are key elements to preparing all students for success in college, careers, and life."

- **Dr. Joe A. Hairston, Superintendent, Baltimore County Public Schools, 2000-present**

"I love the way we learn in Baltimore County."

- **Nicole Mueller, Age 10, Lutherville**

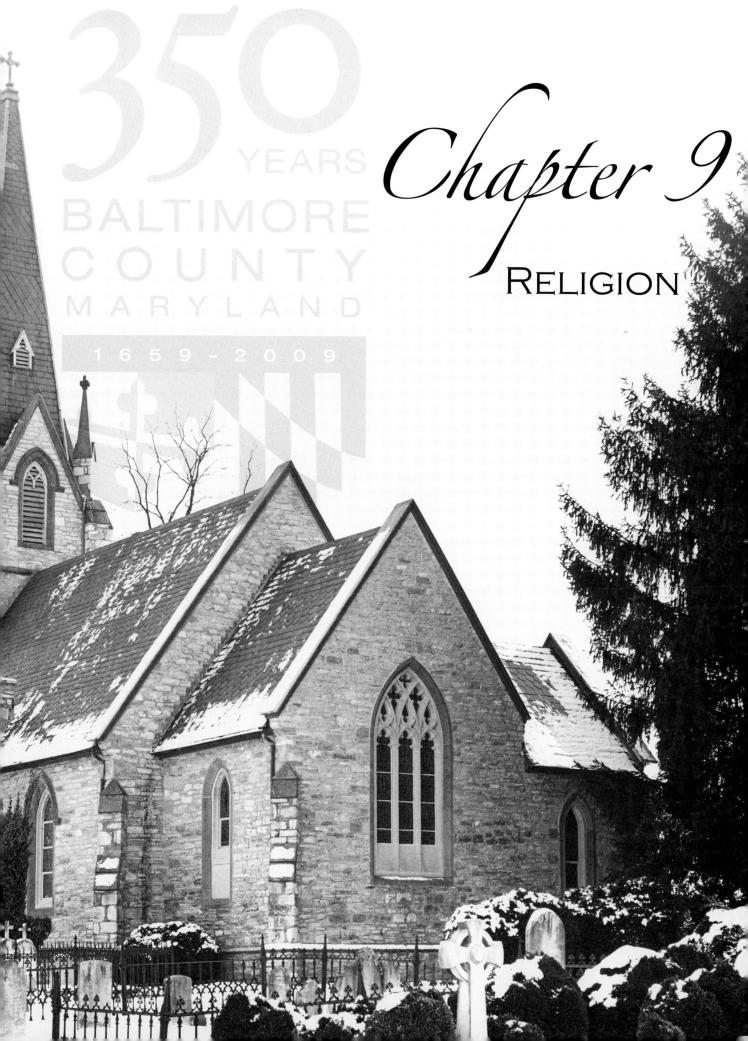

350

YEARS

BALTIMORE

COUNTY

MARYLAND

1659 - 2009

Chapter 9

RELIGION

*I*t is difficult to travel the highways and byways of Baltimore County without passing a house of worship. Some are abandoned and have fallen into ruins, some are in the process of construction or renovation, while others are works of art with congregations and leaders who provide the spiritual and moral grounding for a diverse population.

To understand the religious history of Baltimore County is to understand the religious roots of the colonial experience. With the passage of the Toleration Act of 1654, Maryland's counties were the recipients of religious freedom even though the Act did not live up to its original precepts. Thus, Baltimore County quickly became a place for Anglicans, Protestants, Catholics, Quakers and new denominations like Methodists.

After the passage of the Thirteenth and Fourteenth Amendments to the Constitution, churches became the center of many African American enclaves in towns such as Catonsville, Cowdensville and Towson. The churches not only served the religious needs of the parishioners but they also provided for many social needs in a segregated community. Even to this day, long after the formal end of segregation, African American churches abound, maintaining their community roots and serving as a spiritual center.

Similar to the development of African American churches, many centers of worship were established based on nationality as well as religious affiliation. Russian, Greek and Korean churches are but a few examples of the desire to perpetuate nationalistic and cultural ties associated with faith.

Accordingly, Jewish immigrants settled in Baltimore County and organized into congregations professing Conservative, Orthodox, Reform and Reconstructionist beliefs. As with many other religions, schools supporting their faith and morals were established. They also developed groups designed for fellowship and the improvement of society.

In an era of expanding diversity and expression of beliefs, Baltimore County is home to approximately 300 churches, more than twenty synagogues and at least fifty additional centers of worship professing different beliefs. While ideologies vary, the fundamental belief in a higher power transcends the County's cultural, racial and ethnic differences. As it did before the formation of the United States, religion continues its legacy as a social foundation and a moral compass for the neighborhoods of Baltimore County; a unifying force in a diverse world.

"Religions are many and diverse, but reason and goodness are one."

Elbert Hubbard

St. John's in the Valley Episcopal Church, located on Butler Road in Glyndon, was originally built in 1816; however, it was destroyed by fire on Christmas, 1867. The current church was reconstructed in 1869 by the Westminster firm of Short and Leister. (Photograph courtesy of the Baltimore County Public Library)

Bishop John Emory (1789-1835) was a major figure in the early history of the Methodist Church. He also played a role in the founding of Wesleyan University. Unfortunately, he was killed when he was thrown from his buggy on Reisterstown Turnpike. (Portrait courtesy of the Baltimore County Legacy Web)

A Quaker Meeting House, in Quaker Bottom, was built in 1821 to replace a stone structure on Beaver Dam Road. The new building soon burned but the furniture and 500 book library were saved. The current structure was built in 1866 and was photographed in 1903. Falling into ruins by the mid-twentieth century, the historic structure has been in the process of restoration over the last several decades. (Photograph courtesy of the Maryland State Archives)

The Bosley Methodist Church, located on Thornton Mill Road in Sparks, overlooked an expansive agricultural valley. In 1877, it was the third church to be built on the site. It even used some of the stone from the ruined Thornton Mill for its basement. (Photograph courtesy of John McGrain and the Historical Society of Baltimore County)

Trinity Episcopal Church on Allegheny Avenue remains a Towson landmark having been designed in the mid-1800s by Norris G. Starkweather. (Photograph courtesy of the Baltimore County Public Library)

The diminutive community of Cowdensville, located near Arbutus, is a little known Baltimore County community. Historically African American, this church has served the community since 1857 and has always been led by members of the Williams family. Recently restored, the Baltimore County Office of Community Conservation assisted in the preservation efforts. (Photograph courtesy of John McGrain)

Near the crest of Putty Hill Avenue on Belair Road heading south, Cardinal Gibbons' cavalcade traveled back to his residence at the Basilica in Baltimore City. It is believed that the Archbishop of Baltimore presided over a confirmation at St. Joseph's Church on Sunday, May 20, 1906. (Photograph courtesy of the Historical Society of Baltimore County)

Beginning in 1887 as a Methodist tent city, Emory Grove Campground in Glyndon, quickly experienced Chatauqua-like development, resulting in a complex of frame cottages, auditoria and a forty-room, three-story, mansard-roofed hotel which was built in 1885. Drinking, card-playing and cursing were strictly prohibited. Except for the hotel, which has been closed but restored, the camp remains in use as originally intended. (Photograph courtesy of John McGrain and the Historical Society of Baltimore County)

"Aunt Sarah" Dorsey, a servant, is seen outside the Edmund W. Stable family tent at the Emory Grove campground in Glyndon, circa the 1890s. The Methodist members of the Emory Grove Association rented tents each summer for religious meetings and dismantled them by the end of each season. (Photograph courtesy of the Baltimore County Public Library)

Parishioners of the Perry Hall Methodist Church on Belair Road were gathered for the dedication of their new reed organ, circa the 1880s. Identified are Gibbons Moore with his hand on the organ and his son, George Moore, sitting on the organ stool. (Photograph courtesy of the Baltimore County Public Library)

155

The Halethorpe Methodist Church and the elementary school were the first two non-residential buildings constructed in Halethorpe before 1900. The church served as a house of worship and community center for social activities. Horse drawn carriages were the main form of transportation during this period in Baltimore County. The church stayed in use until 1958 when it was replaced with a larger structure. (Photograph courtesy of the Lanman Family)

The West Liberty United Methodist Church on West Liberty Road in White Hall was erected in 1898 for $7000 replacing an 1819 chapel. For some reason, no marriages were performed in the congregation until 1896. (Photograph courtesy of the Baltimore County Public Library)

A 1912 postcard captured Towson's Church of the Immaculate Conception. The rectory is the structure at the right. (Postcard courtesy of the Baltimore County Public Library)

The first Church of Ascension, which came to be known as the "Church on the Hill," was located on Fairview Avenue in Halethorpe. The photograph of the sanctuary's interior was taken on October 15, 1922. (Photograph courtesy of the Baltimore County Public Library)

A graduation ceremony in 1931 at St. Joseph's Church in Fullerton was photographed by Hebbel Studin. (Photograph courtesy of the Historical Society of Baltimore County)

St. John's Lutheran Church was organized in July 24, 1887 with thirty-two charter members by Reverend Edward Huber. This photograph of the church was taken during the late 1920s or early 1930s. Currently, the intersection of Harford Road and Putty Hill Avenue is surrounded by three churches and each has played a role in the developing community. For the last several years, the combined churches conduct an annual unified prayer service for the Parkville area. (Photograph courtesy of the Greater Parkville Community Council History Committee)

Sister Mary Philomena Micheau led a processional of novice and professed Oblate Sisters of Providence on the grounds of Our Lady of Mount Providence Convent in the mid-1960s. The Oblate Sisters of Providence (OSP) was the first order of Catholic nuns of African descent. (Photograph courtesy of the Oblate Sisters of Providence)

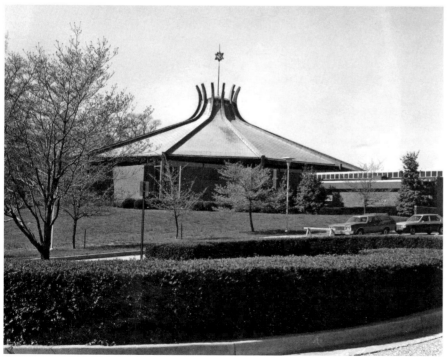

Beth Tfiloh congregation has been a vibrant hub of the Jewish Community since 1921. It has a rich heritage of offering religious services, classes and year-round Jewish programming for children, families, young adults and seniors from all levels of Jewish observance. A day school also offers an extensive K-12 curriculum. In 1964, the Beth Tfiloh congregation replaced its Orthodox Synagogue on Garrison Boulevard with this new modern style synagogue on Old Court Road. With over 1400 members, the congregation is the largest Modern Orthodox Synagogue in America. (Photograph courtesy of the Baltimore County Public Library)

The Beth El congregation was founded in 1948 as the first Conservative Synagogue in Baltimore with the ideals of preserving traditional Jewish values and life while confronting the challenges of modern life. The Beth El synagogue was built in 1960 on Park Heights Avenue in Pikesville. Only three senior rabbis have served the congregation in its entire sixty year history. (Photograph courtesy of the Baltimore County Public Library)

Kippah Ceremony - Children from Beth El Congregation's Early Childhood Education Program gave a "thumbs-up" after completing their Kippah Ceremony. (Photograph courtesy of the Beth El Congregation)

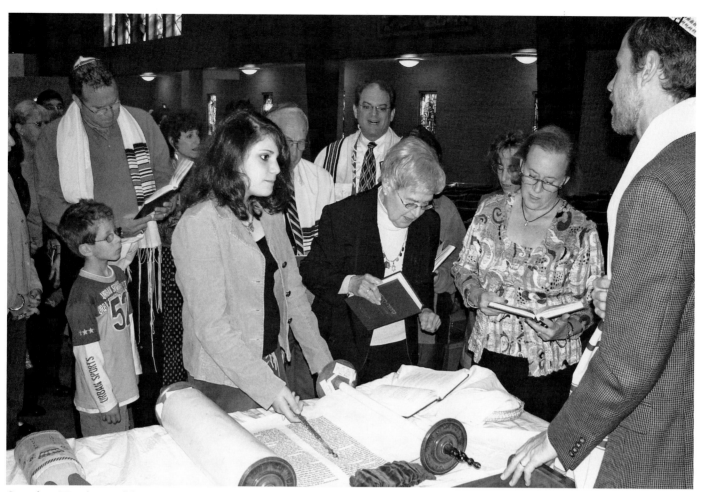

Simchat Torah - Rabbi Steven Schwartz of Beth El Congregation helped lead members of the congregation in the reading of the Torah on Simchat Torah. (Photograph courtesy of the Beth El Congregation)

In 2003, donated clothes and other items were packaged by the Halethorpe-Relay United Methodist Church and sent to several Lithuanian orphanages. (Photograph courtesy of Halethorpe-Relay Methodist Church)

The Men's Flower Mart at the Halethorpe-Relay Methodist Church in 2004 served as an activity to raise money for a variety of community projects. (Photograph courtesy of Halethorpe-Relay Methodist Church)

A ceremony held at the Union Bethel AME Church in Randallstown celebrated the life of Dr. Martin Luther King, Jr. on January 12, 2007. The event also recognized the Content of Character honorees designated by the County's Office of Fair Practices and Community Affairs. The event featured music by the Milford Mill Academy Concert Choir. (Photograph courtesy of the Baltimore County Office of Communications)

At a 2004 worship service held by the Sikh Association in Randallstown, County Executive Jim Smith, spoke about ethnic and religious diversity and how to capitalize on these strengths in Baltimore County. (Photograph courtesy of the Baltimore County Office of Communications)

All Nations Church has served members from several Central American countries. Since the building was built in 1884, at least five different religious denominations have called this church home. Other than the paint scheme, the structure has seen few modifications over the decades. (Photograph courtesy of Dr. Charles J. Kokoski)

Baltimore County Memories . . .

"In the interviews of numerous African Americans who were either born in Granite or resided in Granite, many African Americans attended the Saint Alphonsus Catholic Church. This was because many of the African Americans worked for the Jesuits at Woodstock College, while some were descendants of the slaves of the Jesuits who were brought from the Eastern Shore of Maryland...near the conclusion of the Civil War."

- **Louis S. Diggs, *Surviving in America***

"While Parkville has changed over the years, we still have the same three churches at the intersection of Harford Road and Putty Hill Avenue."

- **Joy Fritsch Piscitelli, Parkville**

"In 1905, a Jewish agriculture colony located on Johnnycake Road was founded by Russian-Jewish immigrants. The purpose was to encourage Jews to move from overcrowded city ghettoes and to diversify the Jewish occupational structure. The colony received a charter under the Hebrew name 'Yaazor,' which means 'He will help'...By the early 1930s, the colony came to an end because people became tired of the hard farming life and returned to the city.... Today, Baltimore County contains a thriving Jewish population supported by many synagogues."

- **Maurice Feldman, Pikesville**

"My brother, sister and I walked to and from the Catholic school, Sacred Heart, daily and would meet our friends along the way. My brother and I were altar boys, and we occasionally had to serve the Mass that was held at 7 a.m. during the week. I remember having to walk to the church (10-15 minutes away) in the cold, dark, winter weather to assist the priest with the daily service, and there might be only a handful of people at the church."

- **Jim Wharton, Mount Washington**

"Our church was organized in 1855 and purchased land in 1889. The first sanctuary burned to the ground in 1968. Our congregation, many of whom are still active, was devastated. We worshipped at the First Lutheran Church on Burke Avenue until a new sanctuary was built. Mt. Calvary stands as a testimony that a 'building' was burned but the 'ministry' to the community remained alive. We are now in our 119th year of worshipping and serving our Almighty God in the Historic East Towson Community and beyond. We built a new sanctuary in 1997 and are building a three-story, state-of-the-art Family Life Center to provide even greater ministry to our community."

- **Reverend Dr. Ann F. Lightner-Fuller, Pastor, Mt. Calvary African Methodist Episcopal Church Towson**

"The church in the African American community was and is the lifeline to survival. Historically out of the church came the school for the Negro children. The church and the school were the places where black preachers, teachers, doctors, lawyers and blue-collar workers were nurtured and taught valuable lessons. If it were not for the church in the community there would not have been a social life or an environment that was supportive of black children. Today the church bridges our past to a new horizon and a future of hope to a new generation."

- **Reverend Sandra E. Demby, *The Hereford Charge***

"Although Lutherville was founded in 1852, it wasn't until the 1870s and 1880s that businesses and professional men began to move there. Those who were Episcopalians had to travel two miles to Towson to worship at Trinity Church. Feeling a need for a meeting place of their own, the Holy Comforter congregation was established in1882 as the 91st Parish/Mission of the Diocese of Maryland…After meeting for a few years in the Town Hall of Lutherville, plans were made for the congregation to have its own home. Having acquired the property at Bellona Avenue and Seminary Avenues construction started in June 1888 and was finished by early autumn. The parish remained small, with only 36 regular communicants by 1932. Construction boomed after World War II with a commensurate increase in the area's population… In 1966, plans for a new church building began to take shape, and ground was broken on June 25, 1967. The building was completed in time for services to be held there on December 22, 1967. By this time, there were 129 young members registered in the Sunday School."

- **Braxton Mitchell, Church of the Holy Comforter Lutherville**

"By 2001, there were numerous African American churches in Randallstown; however, only one such church exists on historic Church Lane whose history dates back almost 200 years. The Church is Union Bethel African Methodist Episcopal Church."

- **Louis S. Diggs, *Surviving in America***

"Jessup Methodist Church in Cockeysville has a tradition of hosting a candle-lighting service on Christmas Eve. This service has been enjoyed for many years by some of the oldest families in Baltimore County."

- **Terrance Powell, Cockeysville**

"Prior to 1839, there were no public religious services in Towsontown, except occasionally a prayer meeting at a private home. In 1839, a Citizens' Committee started a movement to erect a union church to be used by all denominations. Henry B. Chew, owner of Epsom Estate, donated the ground for the Epsom Chapel, which was the exact site of an old arsenal built by General Nathan Towson and occupied by the U.S. Government during the War of 1812 (now the ground for the Towsontown Center)…In 2008, after 50 years at the Hampton Lane location, Towson United Methodist Church celebrated the continuity of family, friends, worship, community and the place from which we launch the mission of our Church. Through dance, music, praise, food, crafts, art, poetry [and] with all the resources and gifts of the Church, we joined with our Towson community in rededicating ourselves to the next 50 years."

- **Pamela B. Mitchell, Chair, 50th Anniversary Committee, Towson United Methodist Church**

"The Lansdowne Volunteer Fire Department and Our Savior Evangelical Lutheran Church are partners in making the community a better place. Along with Reverend Kristi E. Kunkel, we conduct joint-venture rummage sales, Halloween activities and events like a Santa Claus Breakfast. Assistance for families in need is an ongoing effort of our combined work."

- **Donna Kern, President, Lansdowne Volunteer Fire Department**

"Diversity and freedom of expression of one's faith has always been a cornerstone of life in Baltimore County."

- **Joseph Bartenfelder, Baltimore County Councilman, 6th District**

Chapter 10

SERVING THE PUBLIC

*A*s settlements took hold and a government slowly organized at the local level, "Old Baltimore" on the Bush River, in what is now Harford County, became the first County Seat. At the dawn of the eighteenth century, however, the County Seat was moved to the Baltimore County side of Gunpowder Falls at Joppa, where it remained until 1768. Following this locale, for economic and political reasons, the government was relocated to the port of Baltimore Town, now known as Baltimore City. The County Seat remained there until 1851 when Baltimore County and Baltimore City divided into two distinct political jurisdictions. A vote in 1854 placed the government in Towson where it has remained for 155 years.

Over the next century, the County was governed by a Board of Commissioners. However, in November of 1954, the voters elected a Charter Board to draft a proposed Home Rule Charter for the County. The recommendations were approved by the electorate on November 6, 1956 and became effective the next month. The first County Council was elected on January 23, 1957 and the Board of County Commissioners ceased to exist. Since that time, there have been eleven County Executives, ten Democrats and one Republican.

In addition to elected officials and the formal operations of government, essential services to protect life and property were implemented when the Baltimore County Police Department was established in 1874 and the Baltimore County Fire Department was founded in 1881. Other services followed over time including road construction, trash removal and a system of public works.

To further improve the quality of life and make the County a more enjoyable place in which to live, the first public library was opened with private funds in 1915. Since that time, the system has grown to eighteen branches housing more than 1.6 million books and state of the art technology. Along with the libraries, the Department of Recreation and Parks has maintained 190 parks since 1948, supporting the diverse recreational interests of the County's citizens.

While thousands of workers are employed to provide a secure environment, maintain a comfortable way of life and administer critical health care, Baltimore County has also had a distinguished history of volunteer service. Examples of these organizations range from community associations and volunteer fire departments to community assistance groups. Literally hundreds of organizations with thousands of non-paid volunteers give of themselves to improve the quality of life for their neighbors. Thus, from the days when doctors made house calls and horses pulled fire engines, caring people have worked together to make their County a better, safer and more enjoyable place in which to live.

"Never doubt that a small group of thoughtful, committed citizens can change the world; indeed, it is the only thing that ever has."

Margaret Mead

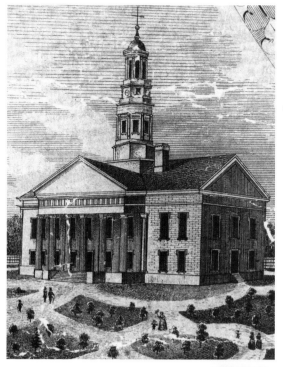

The original main block of the Towson Court House was built in 1854-1856, wings were added in 1910. Additions in 1926 and 1958 completed its current configuration. The center of Baltimore County government was depicted on a rare engraving for a wall map produced by Rogerson & Brown in the 1850s. The engraving shows the three-part spire that was reduced to only one part in 1863. (Engraving courtesy of the Baltimore County Public Library)

This former Stone jail was located on Belair Road, in Kingsville. It was used to confine convicts who worked on County roads. (Photograph courtesy of John McGrain and the Historical Society of Baltimore County)

After Baltimore City was granted separation from Baltimore County in 1851, the County had to relocate all offices and institutions. The Baltimore County Almshouse, later known as the Baltimore County Home, opened in 1872. The Almshouse was home to the County's indigent until 1958. The Historical Society of Baltimore County currently occupies the building in Cockeysville. (Photograph courtesy of the Historical Society of Baltimore County)

The original firehouse of the Pikesville Fire Company at Reisterstown Road and Sudbrook Lane was originally painted white in the late nineteenth century. The one-horse, Gould hand-pump mounted on a spring wagon was acquired in 1896 and carried a hose and other equipment. A watch tower was constructed to the right of the fire-house. (Photograph courtesy of the Baltimore County Public Library)

Edwin George Prince was a ranger for the Forest Reserves in Patapsco Valley. He was also one of the first Park Rangers in Maryland, circa 1900. (Photograph courtesy of the Catonsville Room, Baltimore County Public Library)

Villa Maria at Notchcliff in Glen Arm was established by the School Sisters of Notre Dame for retired and convalescent members of their order. The photograph was taken in 1917 when the structure was relatively new. The property remained under the control of the order until 1984 when it was purchased privately. It was later transformed into Glenn Meadows, a senior living facility. (Photograph courtesy of the Baltimore County Public Library)

Carville Benson along with his father, Oregon Benson were developers and highly active in Baltimore County politics during the first two decades of the twentieth century. Carville was elected to the House of Representatives but eventually lost his seat as a result of his opposition to women's suffrage in 1920. (Photograph courtesy of Special Collections, Albin O. Kuhn Library & Gallery, University of Maryland, Baltimore County)

At the age of twenty-two, James Rittenhouse was elected Baltimore County Sheriff. After two terms at the post, the voters elevated him to the position of County Commissioner in 1877. Rittenhouse served in that capacity for sixteen years. Along with his political career, which was at its height in the 1890s, Rittenhouse also engaged in real estate development and ran a large truck farm. (Photograph courtesy of Special Collections, Albin O. Kuhn Library & Gallery, University of Maryland, Baltimore County)

This official Baltimore County Police car was actually owned by Officer Joseph F. Miller of Parkville during the 1920s. (Photograph courtesy of the Baltimore County Public Library)

In 1926, Baltimore County Judges and lawyers were photographed in Court Room #5 of the Baltimore County Courthouse. Court Room #5 has been restored to its original appearance and is currently used for ceremonial occasions. (Photograph courtesy of the Baltimore County Public Library)

Chief Deputy George B. Marley worked at his desk in the Sheriff's Office in Towson. The calendar hanging on the wall was for the year, 1930. (Photograph courtesy of the Historical Society of Baltimore County)

The former Towson Police Station, located on Washington Avenue, was built in 1926 as a single-story structure and later expanded to a two-floor station in the 1930s. In 2000, the building was auctioned because it was obsolete for police purposes at that time. In private hands, a developer renovated the building and it is currently used for office space. (Photograph courtesy of John McGrain and the Historical Society of Baltimore County)

The Pikesville Fire Department's American La France engine was capable of pumping 750 gallons of water per minute. The engine required a crew of seven men in 1934. (Photograph courtesy of the Historical Society of Baltimore County)

This tiny frame building was constructed in 1932 and served as the Bentley Springs Post Office until it was closed by the cost-conscious Postal Service in 1984. However, its small size had not prevented it from becoming the vital center of community life. Its final Postmistress, Marie Duncan, was the third generation of her family to hold the assignment. Like so many other communities, Bentley Springs had grown since 1838 as a result of the railroad. (Photograph courtesy of John McGrain and the Historical Society of Baltimore County)

On October 3, 1952, vice-presidential candidate Richard Nixon gave a campaign speech in Dundalk. Nixon had lived in Wilson Point for a short time after World War II while in the Navy working with government contractors. (Photograph courtesy of the Dundalk-Patapsco Neck Historical Society Museum)

A crowd gathered, in 1954, for the dedication and opening of the new Parkville Police and Fire Station at Old Harford and Putty Hill Roads. The combination of police and fire services was a model used in the County for several decades prior to the 1960s. (Photograph courtesy of the Baltimore County Public Library)

Walter Myers was the first African American, Baltimore County, Policeman in the 1950s. He served in the Towson area. (Photograph courtesy of Louis Diggs)

Planning for the Cold War Defense of Baltimore, the new Nike Ajax, a liquid-fueled, surface-to-air missile, with a conventional explosive warhead began to replace the old anti-aircraft gun units around the Baltimore area in 1953. A Nike Hercules missile was photographed on its elevator cradle with its launch crew at the Granite, Woodstock, Nike Missile Base Launch Area, Hernwood Road, circa 1960. By 1958, the Army began replacing the Nike-Ajax with nuclear-armed, solid-fueled, Nike-Hercules missiles. Granite became the first National Guard battalion to assume operational control of the nuclear warhead-equipped Nike Hercules missiles until they were banned by the Strategic Arms Limitation Treaty of 1972. Ultimately, the Launch site became a Maryland Police and Correctional Training Commission facility. (Photograph courtesy of the Granite Historical Society Nike Missile Base History Project collection, courtesy of Colonel Joe Zang)

Baltimore County libraries in the 1960s, like the Catonsville branch, housed only printed materials; all records were kept on paper. It would be another few decades before they would obtain computers, digital media and the Internet. (Photograph courtesy of the Catonsville Room, Baltimore County Public Library)

In 1960, the Baltimore County Public Library's Bookmobile parked in front of Randallstown Elementary School on Liberty Road. The Bookmobile was a popular way for books to make their way to the community. (Photograph courtesy of the Baltimore County Public Library)

In 1960, the national headquarters of the Social Security Administration was located in Woodlawn. The complex has expanded dramatically since it was originally built. The Social Security Administration is currently one of the largest employers in the County. (Photograph courtesy of the Historical Society of Baltimore County)

Two months before Senator John F. Kennedy was elected President, he gave a campaign speech on the parking lot of Towson Plaza. Kennedy was flanked by Baltimore County and state politicians. (Photograph courtesy of the Baltimore County Public Library)

Spiro T. Agnew, Baltimore County Executive in 1963, tested a new firebox on Washington Avenue in Towson. Agnew would later serve as Maryland Governor from 1966-1968 and as Vice President of the United States from 1968-1972. However, he ultimately resigned his position as Vice President due to political transgressions. (Photograph courtesy of the Baltimore County Public Library)

While never holding an elected office, Dr. Joseph Thomas was a leading community figure in the southeast section of Baltimore County. Dr. Thomas maintained a medical practice in Turner Station but also owned Edgewater Beach and the Anthony Theater. Thus, he provided African Americans with access to a variety of accommodations in an era of segregation. (Photograph courtesy of the Dundalk-Patapsco Neck Historical Society)

Dedicated in 1965, the Greater Baltimore Medical Center on North Charles Street in Towson cost $14 million to build and was a state-of-the-art facility at the time. Over the life of the hospital, the facility has constantly grown and provided excellent medical care for area residents. (Photograph courtesy of the Baltimore County Public Library)

State Senator James A. Pine addressed an unidentified group during his last campaign in 1974. He was defeated by Donald P. Hutchinson who would ultimately become the County Executive. Political reforms which occurred in 1966, following Supreme Court rulings, changed the number of Baltimore County's state senators from one to eight. Thus, the power of the old Democratic machine diminished as new community organizations became influential and elected candidates supporting a wave of change. (Photograph courtesy of the Heritage Society of Essex and Middle River)

County Executive, Theodore Venetoulis (1974-1978) and Mayor William Donald Schafer worked together to provide improved water quality for Baltimore County and Baltimore City in 1976. (Photograph courtesy of the Baltimore County Public Library)

The classic beauty of the original Baltimore County Courthouse was documented by County Historian, John McGrain, in 1968. (Photograph courtesy of John McGrain and the Historical Society of Baltimore County)

The original Baltimore County Courthouse shared the Towson skyline with the "new" courthouse in 1977. Towson State University, now Towson University, can be seen in the distance. (Photograph courtesy of John McGrain and the Historical Society of Baltimore County)

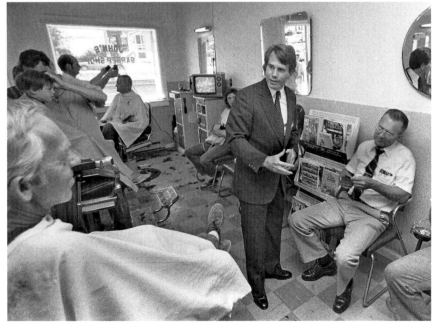

Delegate Tomas Kernan held an impromptu political discussion in John's Barber Shop on Oregon Avenue in Arbutus in May of 1986; a typical grassroots political scene in Baltimore County. (Photograph courtesy of the Baltimore County Public Library)

The Korean-American Community Discussion Group is one of many such organizations that met in an open forum to address issues relating to a specific cultural, national or racial group. Through these dialogues the needs of a diverse population are voiced. (Photograph courtesy of the Baltimore County Office of Communications)

While training between actual emergencies, Baltimore County firemen also contribute to the County in a variety of ways. One such endeavor was a fund-raiser in 2008; the "Fill the Boot" campaign for Muscular Dystrophy. (Photograph courtesy of the Baltimore County Office of Communications)

The Civil Air Patrol participated at the third Waterfront Festival held on May 12, 2007. Events included the arrival of three seaplanes and a unique docking contest. The proceeds from the festival benefited the Marine Trades Association Scholarship Program and the Glenn L. Martin Maryland Aviation Museum. (Photograph courtesy of the Baltimore County Office of Communications)

On May 17, 2007, the annual Memorial Service honoring police officers who lost their lives in the line of duty was held in front of the County Police Monument located in the County Courts Plaza. In over 125 years of service, the Baltimore County Police Department has lost seven officers. (Photograph courtesy of the Baltimore County Office of Communications)

The Emergency Operations Center coordinates a variety of agencies including the Baltimore County Office of Homeland Security and is responsible for the implementation of the Emergency Operations Plan for the County. Emergencies and the Winter Storm Center are major parts of the daily operations of this vital service. (Photograph courtesy of the Baltimore County Office of Communications)

Baltimore County dedicated three new helicopters and the BCPD helicopter hanger at Martin State Airport in 2007. The 10,000 square foot hanger is large enough to provide improved accessibility to flight response. The American Eurocopters provide quicker response times and are the best equipped police helicopters in the U.S. Airborne Law Enforcement community. (Photograph courtesy of the Baltimore County Office of Communications)

Baltimore County Memories . . .

"Timonium was a small village when I began practice. York Road was a two-lane road, and the Harrisburg Expressway was nonexistent. There were three physicians north of Towson: Drs. Elizabeth Sherrill and Walter Kees in Cockeysville, and Dr. Menares France in Parkton. The nearest hospital was Union Memorial. There were many farms in the area, and about 30% of my practice initially consisted of farmers and their families. House calls were the rule rather than the exception. Very few patients were in nursing homes (indeed, there were very few nursing homes because of lack of demand), and all of us made regular house visits to the chronically ill. In addition, emergency calls were usually made at home."

- **Dr. William A. Pillsbury, President, 1957 Baltimore County Medical Association**

"The site where the National Guard building is now on York Road and the Beltway (I-695) was a 90mm anti-aircraft gun site during the Cold War. There were also gun sites at Smith Avenue and Old Pimlico Roads, and Rolling Road just north of Route 40. Other gun sites existed around the city of Baltimore. Later, Nike missile sites were constructed: Granite, Greenspring Avenue at Ridge Road, Jacksonville, Harford Road just north of the Little Gunpowder Falls and on Hawkins Point Road."

- **Claude "Greg" Gregory, Timonium**

"It's been an honor to work within Baltimore County Government since joining the Department of Public Works in 1990. The vast majority of Baltimore County employees are looking for ways to continuously improve service to Baltimore County citizens. Of course, we're not always right or the first to implement a good idea, but in general our concern is genuine and efforts positive and practical...If you're going to invest much, if not most of your waking time working someplace, why not do it somewhere you can contribute and feel good about it? While the exceptions sometimes get more attention, the vast majority of citizens appreciate the job Baltimore County employees do on a day-to-day basis."

- **Charlie Reighart, Baltimore County Department of Public Works/Bureau of Solid Waste Management, Baltimore County Government**

"The Baltimore County government was established by the adoption of the Baltimore County Charter, which the voters approved on November 6, 1956. The County was divided into seven districts with a councilman representing each district and established the three branches of government. While amendments and Charter revisions have been approved over the years, the basic structure of the Charter has remained firm... As a former councilwoman and based upon my experiences in office, I have always recommended that the legislative body write the laws with explicit language addressing the purpose and intent of a bill, thereby eliminating the opportunity for loophole interpretation by judges and the executive branch of government."

- **Berchie Manley, Catonsville**

"I have enjoyed the opportunity to serve the public for the last twenty-six years. Hopefully I have been able to make a difference in making this place a better place for everyone to live, work and play."

- **Joseph Bartenfelder, Baltimore County Councilman, 6th District**

"In serving Baltimore County for more than 55 years as a career and volunteer fireman, I have had the opportunity to witness many changes in our fire service. Over the years, these changes have transformed Baltimore County's fire service into one that is recognized throughout the country as a model for how career and volunteer personnel can work together...our high standards of training and certification have been used across the country to enhance the total fire service. Our citizens can be proud of what we've accomplished."

- **Elwood H. Banister, Baltimore County Fire Chief, Retired**

"Until 1975, the Baltimore County Fire Department retained a formal tradition. A day shift would end at 6 p.m. Daily, at 5:45 p.m., the men who were finishing their shift would retreat to the locker room, remove their working uniform ('Class B') to put on their full dress uniform ('Class A'). They would then stand at attention and face the oncoming night shift for [the] 'pass on' of information...Nowadays, you can leave when your relief arrives, and you can wear what you want to and from work, as long as you put on your Class B uniform before you start your shift--much more flexible and informal."

- **John J. Hohman, Baltimore County Fire Chief**

"Volunteer firefighters began serving in Baltimore County with the founding of the Mechanic Fire Company in 1763. Today, our citizens are served by over 3,000 volunteer men and women who provide skilled fire, rescue and emergency medical care to our citizens."

- **Jim Doran, Volunteer Firefighter**

"Without the Greater Parkville Community Council and its advocates over the years, we would not have such a great place in which to live."

- **Joy Fritsch Piscitelli, Parkville, Carney and Cub Hill**

"Here in Baltimore County government, we are being watchful while carrying on the business of providing the services our citizens depend on."

- **Jim Smith, Baltimore County Executive**

"I love how there are so many parks here, and each one offering something a little different. You can go fishing at one, hiking at another one, or rent a pavilion and have your family reunion at another... There's something for everyone."

- **Lisa Morris, Essex**

"Throughout my career as a police officer, Baltimore County has constantly grown. While this brings law enforcement challenges, the vast majority of its citizens support the police and cooperate to ensure a safe environment of all."

- **Mike Darcey, Patrolman First Class, Wilkens Precinct**

"Baltimore County has a lot of resources and I feel safe."

- **Nada Ibrahim Age 10, Lutherville**

Chapter 11

A Sense of Community

*W*ithout question, a sense of community is difficult to define. It is one of those esoteric aspects of a locale that cannot be physically identified. Though, hard to explain, one can easily feel it when present; sometimes a short walk along a neighborhood street is all that is necessary.

From another perspective, a sense of community can be analyzed in terms of Baltimore County towns, housing developments, subdivisions, enclaves or even single streets. Each community has its own identity which produces and adds a distinctive character to that place and establishes a collective personality unique to the given area that transcends geographical boundaries or political jurisdictions.

While most residents do not ponder these philosophical conundrums, they are aware of its ramifications. It is obvious in the ways that neighbors help each other, socialize and take pride in their homes. Even property values, the strength of a community's political power and the ability to obtain necessary funding for improvements to the infra-structure are impacted by the strength of a community.

Diverse events such as flower competitions in Sparrows Point, sponsored by Bethlehem Steel, at the beginning of the twentieth century or the Maryland State Fair, an occasion which has been referred to as "the best days of summer," reflect a human desire to create social connections that enhance the quality of life in Baltimore County. Although these planned occasions have been critical in building a sense of community there have also been emergencies and disasters like hurricanes Agnes and Isabel which have brought neighbors together in ways that eclipse superficial differences. Such bonds, created from adversity, are lasting.

No matter the time span in Baltimore County, visual representations have captured this illusive concept beyond the written word. While these images are interpreted differently, they speak to Baltimore County's legacy in establishing a sense of community.

"I am of the opinion that my life belongs to the community, and as long as I live it is my privilege to do for it whatever I can."

George Bernard Shaw

RURAL HOMES FOR ALL AT HALETHORPE

HALETHORPE GLENN IMPROVEMENT COMPANY BUILDING ROOM 18 2nd Floor 12 St. Paul St.

A promotional brochure prepared by the Halethorpe Improvement Association Company during the early 1890s included an artist's conception of what Halethorpe would look like in the future. This concept was repeated by many of the communities developed in Baltimore County during this era. (Brochure courtesy of the Halethorpe Heritage Committee)

Charles R. Varley Myers was one of the leading promoters of the town of Halethorpe along with his associates Oregon Benson, Carville Benson and James Rittenhouse. They all had a vision of creating a place that combined quality housing, community organizations, accessible transportation and an area that reflected beauty and tranquility. (Photograph courtesy of Special Collections, Albin O. Kuhn Library & Gallery, UMBC)

For most communities, volunteer fire companies were not only a necessity but an organization that provided social activities. Before World War I, fire stations, like Sparrows Point, were making the transition from horse and hand-drawn equipment to motorized fire trucks. (Photograph courtesy of the Dundalk-Patapsco Neck Historical Society)

This 1912 garden in Sparrows Point was a contender for a prize in the flower contest held by the company officials of the steel plant. The contest was a way in which to beautify the company houses. (Photograph courtesy of the Dundalk-Patapsco Neck Historical Society)

The Suburban Club was at the corner of Park Heights Avenue and Slade Avenue in Pikesville. The club was established in 1903 by members of the affluent German-Jewish community on land leased from Thomas Beale Cockey of neighboring Lyal Park. The building was razed and a new one was erected in 1960. (Photograph courtesy of the Baltimore County Public Library)

Funeral trolley cars carried the deceased to cemeteries. A special container on the side allowed mourners to view the casket through a glass cover. This service was provided in many Baltimore County communities. (Photograph courtesy of the Dundalk-Patapsco Neck Historical Society)

Reverend Paul F. Bloomhardt, the Scoutmaster and Pastor of St. Paul's Lutheran Church, was standing with the Lutherville Boy Scouts on the banks of the Gunpowder River at Paper Mill Road near York Road, circa 1916. (Photograph courtesy of the Baltimore County Public Library)

Sewing and basket weaving were two forms of therapy provided at Spring Grove State Hospital, circa 1915-1920. As of 2009, the facility was in the process of closing after more than century of operation. (Photograph courtesy of the Baltimore County Public Library)

Members of the Odd Fellows lodge stood in front of their headquarters in Catonsville, circa 1910. Jake Rick (back left), Jesse Chamberlain (back center), "Shorty" Ruff (back right), Christian Dehlmann (bottom left) and Daniel Dehlmann (bottom right) all displayed their badges denoting their rank and service. (Photograph courtesy of the Catonsville Room, Baltimore County Public Library)

Built by private initiative, circa 1874, as a Free School for "colored children," the school stayed in use as an educational facility until 1922 when it was purchased by the Union of Brothers and Sisters, Fords Asbury Lodge No.1. Since that time, the Lodge has had a difficult time maintaining the building and has had the building moved back from the edge of busy Philadelphia Road in the Loreley vicinity. (Photograph courtesy of John McGrain and the Historical Society of Baltimore County)

During the Fair of the Iron Horse in 1927, Native Americans dressed in traditional garments, came to worship at Ascension Church in Halethorpe. Father Flanigan and members of the congregation posed with their guests. (Photograph courtesy of the Christian Family)

Master stonemasons Seymour Ruff & Sons, builders of the Fieldstone community, now a County Historic District, constructed the Randallstown Community Center in 1927. In addition to the community bank on the main floor it housed a large performance hall on the third floor. The community of Fieldstone raised $100,000 to fund construction of the building. The restoration of the building was an example of a concerted effort by a community to preserve structures of architectural and cultural significance. (Photograph courtesy of John McGrain and the Historical Society of Baltimore County)

Seated at the left, Eleanor Roosevelt, wife of President Franklin D. Roosevelt, visited a friend, Louise Bahr, seated in the middle. The visit took place in Lansdowne during 1932. (Photograph courtesy of the Baltimore County Public Library)

While this windmill appears to be located in the Netherlands, it is actually part of The Cloisters, an eclectic estate with a thirty-three room mansion. The estate was built of Butler stone between 1930 and 1932 by Sumner Parker. The family also obtained a large collection of American and European art and artifacts. The Cloisters has been a popular children's museum since 1972. (Photograph courtesy of John McGrain and the Historical Society of Baltimore County)

The 1931 Timonium Fair Midway was considerably smaller than its contemporary counterparts. However, the rides and the games have always been a main attraction at the Fair. (Photograph courtesy of the Historical Society of Baltimore County)

A photographer captured family memories at the 1933 Maryland State Fair. (Photograph courtesy of the Historical Society of Baltimore County)

Baltimore County Public Schools provided a display at the 1949 Maryland State Fair in Timonium which focused on the growth of Baltimore County after World War II and the corresponding growth of the school system. The display was prophetic considering the expansion that was predicted for the next several decades. (Photograph courtesy of the Historical Society of Baltimore County)

Maryland State Fair officials congratulated two female contest winners, circa 1950. (Photograph courtesy of the Historical Society of Baltimore County)

In a more sedate and simplistic time just before World War II, Baltimore County police officer Joseph F. Miller had time to talk with a young citizen along the shopping district of Parkville. *Note the lack of sophisticated electronic or protective devices carried by Officer Miller. (Photograph courtesy of the Baltimore County Public Library)

Famed Metropolitan Opera singer Rosa Ponselle retired from the stage in 1937 and subsequently married a son of Mayor Howard W. Jackson of Baltimore. She built Villa Pace, a distinctive Mediterranean style mansion overlooking Green Spring Valley Road. She later became founder and patron of the Baltimore Opera Company and was a tireless supporter of the arts throughout the Baltimore area. (Photograph courtesy of Jacques Kelly)

Camp Puh' Tok, operated by the Salvation Army in Monkton, provided unique summer experiences for boys from the 1940s to the 1960s. Baltimore County Public Schools also provided students with outdoor experiences at the camp. (Photograph courtesy of the Historical Society of Baltimore County)

World War I and World War II veterans march with pride in a VFW parade in Towson, circa the 1950s. During the Red Scare, when there was an intense fear of communism, patriotism was an important issue. (Photograph courtesy of the Historical Society of Baltimore County)

The Baltimore County Teacher's Christmas Chorus performed a holiday concert in 1952 at Pickersgill, a Towson home for senior citizens. (Photograph courtesy of the Baltimore County Public Library)

Hurricane Agnes was one of the most devastating natural disasters to hit the Baltimore area in decades. While the destruction was massive, as seen in Owings Mills in 1972, the community quickly recovered with the help of private, local, state and federal agencies. (Photograph courtesy of the Louise B. Goodwin Research Room, Reisterstown Branch, Baltimore County Public Library)

The members of the Banneker Senior Center, in the 1980s, enjoyed good fellowship while having the chance to discuss the local issues of the day. (Photograph courtesy of the Balti-more County Public Library)

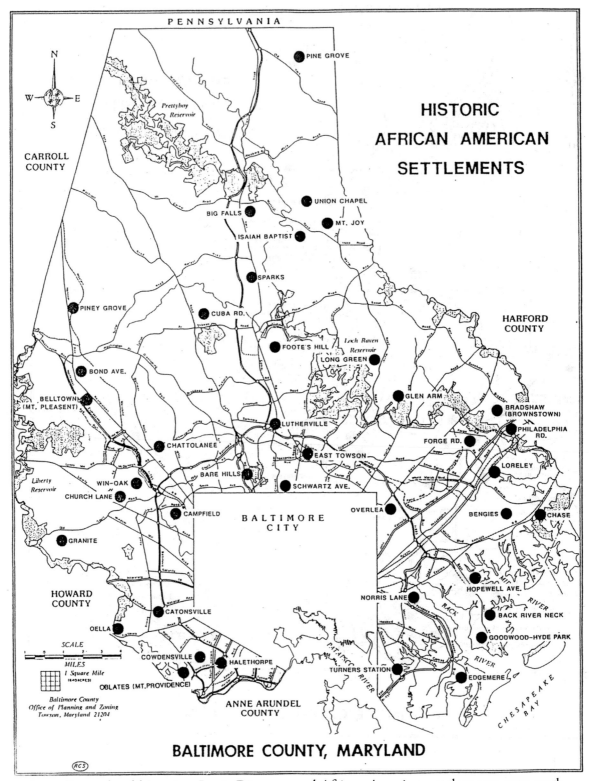

HISTORIC AFRICAN AMERICAN SETTLEMENTS

BALTIMORE COUNTY, MARYLAND

According to local historian, Louis Diggs, several African American settlements were established during Baltimore County's early history. As communities grew during the twentieth century, some developed in a more integrated fashion than others. (Map courtesy of Baltimore County Office of Planning and Zoning)

Louis Rukeyser (left), who hosted the Maryland Public Television program Wall Street Week, spoke with Raymond K. K. Ho, then President of the Broadcasting Company in 1988. Maryland Public Television opened in Owings Mills on September 28, 1969. (Photograph courtesy of Maryland Public Television)

In 2007, the Department of Social Services and the Annual Campership Project raised enough money to send ninety-three children to camp for two weeks. The program was extended to 150 children in 2008. Members of the Middle River Boys & Girls Club participated in these productive summertime activities. (Photograph courtesy of the Baltimore County Office of Communications)

At the Catonsville Senior Center, a program was held in the fall of 2006 to educate citizens on the issues of Medicare and the Prescription Drug Plan. The Baltimore County Department of Aging conducted nineteen of these sessions throughout the County in an effort to be responsive to the needs of senior citizens. (Photograph courtesy of the Baltimore County Office of Communications)

Young girls demonstrated various aspects of Indian cultural heritage. These activities were a part of the Ethnic Diversity Advisory Council's efforts to provide cultural awareness and to support cultural diversity throughout the County. (Photograph courtesy of the Baltimore County Office of Communications)

Starting in 1928, the Relay Day Festival is an example of how small towns in Baltimore County have promoted their heritage through community fairs. Thus, local citizens have fun while passing on time-honored traditions to future generations. (Photograph courtesy of Bill Hermann and the Relay Improvement Association)

This Relay structure had originally been built as a volunteer fire house but has been used as a library, home to a variety of community organizations and currently as the headquarters for the Relay Improvement Association. The Relay Town Hall functions as the heart of the community. (Photograph courtesy of Bill Hermann and the Relay Improvement Association)

On November 10, 2008, guest speaker, retired Colonel James F. Coleman of the United States Air Force, announced Baltimore County's plan to change the name of Towson Courts Plaza to Patriot Plaza in honor of Baltimore County Veterans. The new plaza will feature flags representing every branch of the United States Armed Services with plaques for each branch inserted in the walkway. (Photograph courtesy of the Baltimore County Office of Communications)

Baltimore County Memories . . .

"Victory Villa Community Center had live bands, dances, craft meetings, bridge clubs and other social activities [during and after World War II]... There was a sense of belonging."

- Ray and Marge Barhight, Middle River Oral History Project

"Arbutus --The definition of a small town on the edge of a major city... Your neighbors would be 'in the know' about everything from the participants in the latest school fight to your latest date."

- Robert L. Ehrlich Jr., Governor of Maryland, 2002-2006

"What better way of establishing a community legacy than by volunteering at community events, establishing Scout troops and membership in a service club. Building libraries, recreational centers and religious organizations also create a community legacy for today and for the future."

- Mary Lou Hastry, Catonsville

What I find the most interesting is the small-town mentality of such a large metropolitan area.

- Micah Kleid, Beth El Congregation of Baltimore

"Parkville, Carney and Cub Hill still have that 'Old Time Feel' of a proud, caring community... Double Rock Park is still a great place to go, the Historic Parkville Park will always grace Taylor Avenue, and the sense of pride in community can still be felt."

- Joy Fritsch Piscitelli, Parkville, Carney and Cub Hill

"Great schools, strong communities, steady and sure finances, miles of beautiful farmland, parks, streams and the Chesapeake Bay, our people: Add it all up; there's no better place."

- David Carroll, Director of Sustainability Baltimore County Government

"We know our neighbors... Living in Relay is like being in a time warp."

- William Hermann, Relay

"When I first heard the quote 'It takes a village to raise a child' my first thought was Lutherville from years ago. It was a safe, secure, loving community of people who looked out for each [other]. Everyone knew who we were or who our parents, grandparents, aunts [and] uncles were. We could knock on any door if we needed help or had a problem. And what fun we all had during those growing-up years--how nice that we all still keep in touch with one another."

- Nancy Jane Harrell Stickles, Cockeysville

"Everybody knew everybody...Everybody was friendly...My mother called on her neighbors and friends. She would make blackberry juice from the blackberry bushes at our house.

- Margaret Klein Weimeister, Halethorpe

"I love Baltimore County, and I am so proud to still be a member of the wonderful community."

- April N. Goldring, Hereford

"I like being in Relay because of the people."

- Faith Hermann, Relay

"With the numerous historic African American communities in Baltimore County, whose histories had not been documented, I feel so honored to have published eight books on the histories of these highly significant communities."

- Louis S. Diggs, Catonsville and Owings Mills

"I love Baltimore County because of the friendly people."

- Lacey Parker, Age 10, Lutherville

"Dundalk is the only community that I know that celebrates Independence Day with one of this County's largest traditional parades, fireworks, three-day Heritage Fair celebration--and still has time for family picnics on the Fourth of July."

- Bob Staab, Dundalk

"Our part of the County consisted of three small neighborhoods: English Counsul, Rosemont and Baltimore Highlands. The neighborhood began at the Baltimore City line and ended at the Patapsco River. Annapolis Road was dotted with ponds and a walk…was a delightful experience. The countryside was covered with honeysuckle."

- Beatrice "Betty" Laukaitis Wassermann, Catonsville

"Here in Baltimore County, the diversity of our communities is one of our strongest assets…Ethnic and cultural festivals like these are a great opportunity for citizens to take pride in their traditions and history and have a good time too."

- Jim Smith, Baltimore County Executive

"I love Baltimore County because of the safety, the choices, the communities and the schools."

- Nicole Mueller, Age 10, Lutherville

"I grew up in Sudbrook Park and the community would have a 4th of July parade where we would decorate our bikes in red, white and blue and ride through the neighborhood to the park for judging of the best decorated bike."

- Candace L. Croswell, Sudbrook Park

"You knew everybody. It was a friendly place. I always felt very proud to show my friends Halethorpe."

- Helene Scott, Halethorpe

"Today, Perry Hall still has that hometown feel. It's big and growing but proud of its history and determined to keep a neighborly feel."

- David Marks, Perry Hall

"Schwartz Avenue in East Towson is a small but close-knit community of homeowners. People help each other when the need arises. The residents also protect each other through an informal community watch. Schwartz Avenue truly has a sense of community."

- McCanner Perry, East Towson

"I find it incredibly fascinating how the citizens in our communities energetically and optimistically approach each conflict with a vigor and passion that is second to no one."

- Jordan Hadfield, Main Street Manager, Dundalk Renaissance Corporation

350 YEARS
BALTIMORE
COUNTY
MARYLAND
1659-2009

Chapter 12

CONFLICT & COOPERATION

"*It was the best of times. It was the worst of times.*" While Charles Dickens was assessing France before its Revolution, the same words could also be used to describe the triumphs and travails of Baltimore County.

In the first decades of the County's existence, issues of survival, land patents and religion were the source of most disputes. However, cooperation between farmers and their association with millers were examples of economic partnerships which were beneficial to both parties and the power of working together transcended most differences.

As society progressed, growing pains were inevitable regarding personal and civil rights, labor issues, servitude, slavery and divergent political ideologies. Conversely, cooperation can also be documented through myriad acts of kindness and a willingness of individuals and groups to make Baltimore County a better place in which to live.

One of the most enduring themes of controversy throughout Baltimore County's long history has involved issues regarding working conditions and compensation. Discord between labor and management has manifested itself in the forms of negotiations, protests, strikes and even violence. However, positive resolutions to these conflicts have usually allowed both parties to prosper.

While most events involving conflict and cooperation never made the nightly news, some events have placed Baltimore County in the national spotlight. One such example was the burning of draft records by the Catonsville Nine during the era of Vietnam; an event which crystallized attitudes about the unpopular conflict.

Like the past, in recent years the usage of land has been a source of great discussion along with the issues of economic development. Partnerships between the Baltimore County Government and private enterprise have created such endeavors as urban renaissance projects with thirteen Commercial Revitalization Districts now designated throughout the County. Through these efforts, lively main streets with renovated shopping areas and dynamic town centers are replacing aging strip malls. In addition, new tax credits are available to help maintain and restore historically significant properties and to encourage construction of high performance, environmentally friendly, "green" buildings.

In retrospect, Baltimore County has often been at the vanguard of change while at other times it has had to work hard just to catch up to societal norms. Conflict, frequently the catalyst for change, tested the resolve of its citizens and made the County stronger as growth took place. Thus, rather than being a dilemma, these interactions have forged Baltimore County's collective personality and has defined who it is; a work in progress.

"We must learn to live together as brothers or we are going to perish together as fools."

Martin Luther King, Jr.

Lively political debate has always been a part of life in Baltimore County as this sketch study portrays. The work, titled "Election Scene in Catonsville, 1845" was done by prominent artist Alfred Jacob Miller. The piece currently resides in the Museum of Fine Arts, Boston. It is believed that Miller was inspired by the political debates surrounding the election of James K. Polk. (Sketch courtesy of the Catonsville Room, Baltimore County Public Library)

Greenspring slave quarters, located on Valley Road, were owned in the late-eighteenth and early-nineteenth centuries by the Moale family, who remained slaveholders long after the decline of the tobacco economy in the County. They held eleven slaves in 1798 and the number increased to thirteen by 1850. (Photograph courtesy of John McGrain and the Historical Society of Baltimore County)

Prospect Hall slave quarters, located on Kanes Road, Long Green Valley, serve as a reminder of a failed attempt at tobacco farming in the Green Spring Valley. The last owner before the Civil War was a Mennonite, who faithful to his religion, banned slavery from his property, thus, representing the difference of thought in Baltimore County over the issue of slavery. (Photograph courtesy of John McGrain and the Historical Society of Baltimore County)

Martin Fugate slave quarters, located on Troyer Road, was a tiny structure by today's standards, 18'x 24", however, it was considered a respectable dwelling for the end of the eighteenth century when the majority of County residents were living in primitively constructed log buildings. It is not known how many slaves were housed in this structure. (Photograph courtesy of John McGrain and the Historical Society of Baltimore County)

During the Civil War, Greenleaf Whittier Sawyer served in the Union Army as a private in the 29th Maine Infantry and was wounded at the battles of Cedar Creek and Cedar Mountain. After the war, he came to Baltimore, circa 1872, in search of work and he stayed for the remainder of his life. Sawyer was a gravedigger for Loudon Park Cemetery and assisted in the burial of Confederate and Union soldiers alike. It was his belief that they all deserved respect as war veterans. (Drawing courtesy of the Lanman family)

Following secret deals with Baltimore City, legal suits and actions by the General Assembly, the century old mill town of Warren was purchased by Baltimore City for one million dollars. The town was then destroyed and flooded in 1922 to create Loch Raven Reservoir, the primary source of drinking water for metropolitan Baltimore. Nine hundred residents were displaced by this controversial decision. (Photograph courtesy of the Baltimore County Public Library)

Because of segregation, Dr. Joseph H. Thomas purchased Edgewater Beach in Turner Station so that African Americans had a place for recreation. He also purchased the Anthony Theater for the same reason. This photograph was taken before World War II when swimming pools and other amusements were also segregated. It was not until the 1960s that the laws changed to eliminate segregation. (Photograph courtesy of Louis Diggs)

Young Margaret Williams, who lived in the African American community of Cowdensville, wanted to attend Catonsville High School in the 1930s. Since African Americans could not attend Catonsville High and a high school curriculum was not available in the "colored" school, her parents hired Thurgood Marshall. While the court case was lost in 1939, Baltimore County ultimately did add high school programs in the African American schools for the first time and Thurgood Marshall gained invaluable experience that helped prepare him for a position as a justice on the Supreme Court. (Photograph courtesy of Louis Diggs)

Joseph V. Kahl operated a hidden still on the Gunpowder River during Prohibition. Later, he owned Kahl's Bar located in the 9600 Block of Belair Road. (Photograph courtesy of the Kahl Family)

John Albert Hawkins Sr. married Amy Jane Brooks and together they became leading citizens in Halethorpe. Mrs. Hawkins was active in community affairs and community organizations while Mr. Hawkins was a labor organizer for the AFL-CIO. (Photograph courtesy of Donald Hawkins)

During World War II, German and Italian prisoners of war were housed at local prison camps in Baltimore County. In Catonsville, these prisoners worked on local farms until the end of the war. As the prisoners were well treated, no known escapes or disruptive events were recorded. (Photograph courtesy of the Catonsville Room, Baltimore County Public Library)

This vast, 22-room mansion named Filtston was built in Glencoe for Edward Austen, a New York businessman who returned to the County in 1881 to establish one of the largest dairy farms in Maryland. However, the structure was most unique in that it was used before World War II by the War Department's Office of Special Services, which conducted top secret classes and field exercises for training spies to operate behind enemy lines. (Photograph courtesy of John McGrain and the Historical Society of Baltimore County)

Adolph C. Birgel served as a Ranger at Omaha Beach. (Photograph courtesy of the Birgel Family)

Talbert "Jock" Dett lived on Bond Avenue in Reisterstown. He was a member of the 10th Calvary during World War II; a part of the famed Buffalo Soldiers units formed after the Civil War to protect wagon trains, pioneers and property in the west. The units were disbanded in the 1950s when the military was integrated. After World War II, Dett became a blacksmith and a highly successful horse trainer in the Baltimore area. (Photograph courtesy of Louis Diggs)

During his military service, Sgt. William C. Doyle was awarded a variety of medals including a Bronze Star, Purple Heart and Presidential Unit Citation. Sergeant Doyle served at Normandy, D Plus 1 (the day after D-Day). (Photograph courtesy of William C. Doyle)

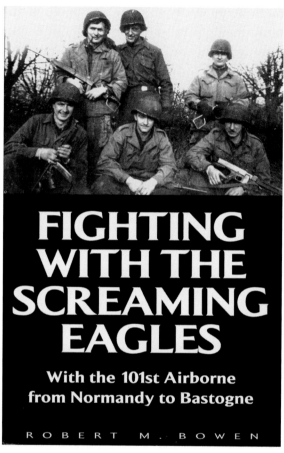

Sergeant Robert Bowen fought with the Screaming Eagles, 101st Airborne Division. He participated in D-Day and the Battle of the Bulge. Sergeant Bowen (bottom right) received the Bronze Star, two Purple Hearts and the Prisoner of War Medal. He later wrote the book entitled Fighting with the Screaming Eagles which chronicled his military exploits. (Photograph courtesy of Robert Bowen)

Lt. Howard McNamara was part of the invasion armada at Normandy on D-Day. (Photograph courtesy of Howard McNamara)

Donald Hawkins (right) and John Albert Hawkins (left) grew up in Halethorpe and served in the Army during the Korean War. Both veterans returned to their hometown after serving their Country. (Photograph courtesy of Donald Hawkins)

Educating young children about community and personal safety has always been a priority in Baltimore County. This group of kindergartners learned important safety tips from the Catonsville Fire Department in the 1950s. (Photograph courtesy of the Catonsville Room, Baltimore County Public Library

Ernestine Boston (second from the right) and Phyllis Randall (third from the right) demonstrated against Five Oaks Swimming Pool on Frederick Road, Catonsville in August, 1963. While the laws eventually changed concerning open accommodations for all citizens, Five Oaks Swimming Pool transitioned to a private club so that membership could still be restricted. (Photograph courtesy of Louis Diggs)

John Leonard Moxley, custodian of the building where the Selective Service office was located, surveyed a broken window. Mrs. Morsberger, a draft board employee, accidentally broke the window when the phone she tried to use to call the police was grabbed by one of the Catonsville Nine. (Photograph courtesy of the Catonsville Room, Baltimore County Public Library)

On May 17, 1968, several hundred draft records were burned with homemade napalm in protest against the war in Vietnam by a group that came to be called "The Catonsville Nine." The charred remains of Catonsville's draft records set off a firestorm of debate on the issue of the military draft and the Vietnam War. The act of civil disobedience marked intensified protests across the nation, which ultimately led to changes in overall public support for the war. (Photograph courtesy of the Catonsville Room, Baltimore County Public Library)

"Guilty but Happy" was the headline for this photograph when it appeared in local and national newspapers. Jean Walsh, local Catonsville historian, took this photograph at the Wilkens Avenue Police Station. She asked the incarcerated group if she could take their picture and was amazed at how receptive they were. This is believed to be the first photograph of the group after the burning of the draft records. The nine defendants were tried and found guilty. As a group, they received eighteen years of jail time and a twenty-two thousand dollar fine. However, Father Daniel Berrigan and Father Phillip Berrigan gained national recognition for their actions. (Photograph courtesy of the Catonsville Room, Baltimore County Public Library)

Political rallies and sit-ins were a part of campus life during the 1960s. Most were peaceful like this one at UMBC in front of the Hillcrest building. (Photograph courtesy of Special Collections, Albin O. Kuhn Library & Gallery, University of Maryland, Baltimore County)

The construction of Route 95 was a major undertaking which created both conflict and cooperation. As can been seen from the two photographs of the Arbutus, Halethorpe and Lansdowne areas, the landscape was radically altered with hundreds of acres consumed for the massive project. Houses in the path of the roadway were bought and demolished under the state and federal project. Feelings about the impact of the highway are still mixed after more than twenty-five years. (Photographs courtesy of the Baltimore County Office of Planning and Zoning)

The photograph above was taken in 1961. The photograph to the right was taken circa 1980. (Photographs courtesy of the Baltimore County Office of Planning and Zoning.

Firemen posted signs comparing the Stump Dump Fire with Desert Storm. Granite residents protested James Jett's burning of tree stumps on his Patapsco Valley Tree Farm and as the fire got out of control and burned underground for months, the cost to taxpayers escalated. The smell and smoke permeated through many neighboring communities. Eventually, legal action was taken and the fire ultimately extinguished. (Photograph courtesy of Baltimore County Public Library)

Goucher College, which was founded as a women's college in 1885, voted to admit men to its undergraduate ranks in May 1986. Trustees who gathered in the Alumnae House for the historic vote were met by hundreds of student protesters, many of whom carried signs and wore T-shirts emblazoned with the message "Better Dead Than Coed." Despite such a proclamation, Goucher is currently a thriving liberal arts college with nearly 1,500 students; approximately one-third of whom are male. (Photograph courtesy of Goucher College)

In the 1980s, excavation occurred at Benjamin Banneker's cabin, located near Oella. The house burned down during Banneker's funeral. Restoration of historical sites such as this help to maintain the County's sense of heritage. (Photograph courtesy of the Baltimore County Public Library)

The economic and the political policies relating to steel production in this country at the beginning of the twenty-first century are captured on the back of a steel worker's jacket. For him and many others, this is not a philosophical debate; it is a matter of survival. (Photograph courtesy of Bill Barry, Director of Labor Studies on the CCBC Dundalk campus)

A rally in Dundalk demonstrated activism at the grass roots level. (Photograph courtesy of Bill Barry, Director of Labor Studies on the CCBC Dundalk campus)

The Dundalk YMCA was constructed during 1949-50 to meet the expanding needs for community services and recreational facilities. Threatened with destruction circa 2000, the survival of this building has been a striking testament to the community's intense love for the facility and the County's support to restore and re-use treasured buildings. The structure now serves as a community center. (Photograph courtesy of John McGrain and the Historical Society of Baltimore County)

The designation of English as the national language was a major campaign issue for this local candidate circa 2006. (Photograph courtesy of Bill Barry, Director of Labor Studies on the CCBC Dundalk campus)

While other buildings previously served as Catonsville High School, this famous Catonsville landmark was built in 1924. After seven decades of service, it was slated for demolition. Only after a protracted effort by the community was the central portion of the building saved and restored. It is now used for County offices and community facilities. Many Catonsville residents consider this building a testament to grass roots political power. (Photograph courtesy of John McGrain and the Historical Society of Baltimore County)

In an effort to improve the environment through recycling, Baltimore County established a permanent electronics recycling collection site in Cockeysville. The site, which began operation in 2006, collected more than a million pounds of electronics in its first year of operation. Collecting electronics for recycling and proper disposal will keep hazardous materials such as mercury, lead, cadmium and arsenic out of local landfills. (Photograph courtesy of the Baltimore County Office of Communication)

Like hurricane Agnes, the ravages of Isabel in the fall of 2003 caused widespread damage. However, residents quickly pitched in to help each other cleanup from the storm surge. Unfortunately, there have been lasting effects in terms of the economic and social impact. (Photograph courtesy of the Baltimore County Office of Communications)

Adopting a road is one way community members have banded together to improve the environment and beautify the area around their homes. Along with individuals, various organizations, fraternities and businesses have combined efforts in order to make a difference. (Photograph courtesy of the Catonsville Room, Baltimore County Public Library)

Taking a weekend to "lift a hand" and improve the aesthetic value of a neighborhood is a simple yet profound act which not only enhances the environment, it improves interactions between neighbors and creates a positive community perception. (Photograph courtesy of the Catonsville Room, Baltimore County Public Library)

Baltimore County Memories . . .

"The Home Interest Club, established [in] 1904, validates you and puts family and homemaking on a different plane."

- **Betsey Cummings, White Hall**

"I remember the flood of 1933 – I was eleven. It was at the end of the summer and most seasonal people had gone back to the city. Quite a few people came to our farm to get drinking water because their wells had been contaminated by the flood waters.

- **Roay Ann McNamara, Seneca Creek / Middle River**

"I must say that life here in Halethorpe has been a wonderful experience. Here I found peace, a neighborhood that is friendly by all, white and African American. We never had racial problems. As children, we always played together and just had good times together."

- **Donald Hawkins, Halethorpe**

"My most significant memory of World War II was seeing prisoners of war work the farmland that was part of the operation of Wilton Farm Dairy – now part of a shopping center on Wilkens Avenue. The men had a large orange "POW" stamped on the back of their uniforms. They were brought to the farm every morning and worked until sundown. A large lunch was prepared for these German workers every day by the owners of the dairy, and one can assume that they were treated kindly by the George J. Zaiser family, owners of the Wilton Farm Dairy since 1881."

- **Edith E. Robinson, Kensington**

"Martin's [during WWII] was called a 'boys town'…Initially, the men didn't think we could do the job, but then found out women were better at certain jobs, especially with small parts."

- **Marge Katonka, Middle River Oral History Project**

"I worked in the welding, machine, sheet metal and nuclear departments at Martin's…Someone's life depends on you and I took my work seriously."

- **Evan Bradey, Middle River Oral History Project**

"Conflict abounded in Baltimore County Democratic party politics in the post-war decades. Until the late 1950s, the local Republican Party was largely irrelevant, but Democratic factions warred among themselves almost ceaselessly. Cooperation briefly existed among them, however, when Chris Kahl (my father) became the first elected County Executive with the support of the disciples of 'Iron Mike' Birmingham, who had become the first Executive by virtue of his being the last chairman of the Board of County Commissioners when the Charter became effective in 1956. However, the normalcy of conflict returned when Birmingham, unhappy with the decline of his influence, then opposed Kahl in 1961 and won the Democratic primary for Executive, only to lose to Ted Agnew, who had picked up considerable support from many of the Kahl faction of Democrats."

- **Christian M. Kahl, Timonium**

"As far as I am concerned, growing up in Parkville was great during the 1950s and 60s. You could leave your door unlocked and not be afraid of someone robbing you.

- **Rocco Rotondo, Parkville**

[After the holidays, Sudbrook Park] would close an intersection and have a Christmas tree burning, and all the neighbors would bring their Christmas trees for a big bonfire and celebration."
- **Candace L. Crosswell, Sudbrook Park**

"Growing up in the 1950s and early 60s in Parkville, I can see the many changes through the years. The Colony Theatre is now the VFW, the farms are gone, as well as a lot of the wooded areas... Parkville has changed from a country to a suburban community."
- **Joy Fritsch Piscitelli, Parkville, Carney and Cub Hill**

"There were national events during the late 1960s which caused problems in every community, including Baltimore County. The Vietnam War and the assassination of Dr. Martin Luther King caused historic reactions in many urban areas of the country. The riots touched Baltimore City and caused problems in some of the high schools in Baltimore County. This was the backdrop of changes that were occurring in the Baltimore metropolitan area."
- **Dr. Anthony Marchione, Superintendent, Retired, Baltimore County Public Schools**

In 1964, there was a food strike. The major food chains closed their doors as a result of a union workers' strike. Eddie's, an independent grocery store, was one of few places open where you could buy food. It was a wild, wild experience, but it felt like we helped the entire community."
- **Frank and Mary Ellen Evans, Catonsville**

"Some thirty-five years ago, I learned an enduring lesson about conflict and cooperation at home, with my father, Charles W. Springer. During the heat of great social strife over a terrible war, and at a time when he was--at least to my teenage eyes--a rigidly conservative patriot and veteran, we sat together in the kitchen listening to the radio news. That day's story was about a son's desertion from military service in Vietnam and the father's subsequent repudiation of the son. Eyeing the precipice of coming change and risk on many levels, I asked my father if that rupture in relationship could ever happen to us. His answer more than satisfied my fear and has echoed since through years of personal and professional community building and peace-making: 'You will always be my son.' His gift that day was to help me see that unconditional regard for one another, in families and beyond, is big enough to heal the most bitter of divides."
- **John C. Springer, Parkville**

"The Perry Hall Improvement Association protested a trailer camp on Cliffvale Avenue, junk yards, a race track for midget cars, apartment projects and--on many occasions--the erection of filling stations in an area already saturated with them."
- **Carroll Dunn, History of the Perry Hall Improvement Association**

"Name any community in Baltimore County and you can identify a core group of volunteers who have individually and collectively spent hours preserving photographs/ memorabilia and oral and written histories about their neighborhood."
- **Barbara Yingling, Past-President, The Historical Society of Baltimore County**

"Baltimore County has been my home since the age of 5 years. The close-knit communities on the southwest area of Baltimore County have provided support, in both my growth and that of my family. I take great pride in living in Baltimore County and especially Catonsville. So many fun times are part of the indelible memories of my life."
- **Sam Moxley, Baltimore County Councilman, 1st District**

350

YEARS

BALTIMORE

COUNTY

MARYLAND

1659 – 2009

Chapter 13

JUST FOR FUN

Consumed with survival, our founding generations had little time for fun and frolic. However, as Baltimore County grew and mechanization reduced work loads, free time increased and people learned to entertain themselves on their own farms and in their local communities. Thus, with each passing generation, the people of Baltimore County have found myriad ways in which to find pleasure and celebrate life.

While neighborhood organizations, churches and clubs provided much of the initial socialization, private enterprises soon realized how to capitalize on the business of fun. Various companies devised such sources of entertainment as Bay Shore, Gwynn Oak and Riverview amusement parks. Movie theaters like the Alpha, Strand and Towson also allowed an escape from reality. In addition to these forms of enjoyment, private golf courses and tennis clubs tested the skills of avid sportsmen.

The County government, aware of a growing interest in leisure opportunities after World War II, initiated the Department of Recreation and Parks in 1949. Since that time, hundreds of programs, including individual and team sports, arts and crafts, social clubs and special events have been provided through a cooperative effort with forty-four volunteer Recreation and Parks Councils throughout the County. The Department, responsible for the parklands and open spaces, shares a joint use agreement with the public schools to maximize community participation. Under the direction of the Department of Aging, nineteen senior centers located throughout the County serve as focal points for programs, activities and services specifically for the mature constituency.

In addition to commercial and governmental participation in recreation, colleges and universities built sports complexes including swimming pools, tracks and field houses for their students and alumni. However, none is more impressive than the Johnny Unitas Stadium located on the campus of Towson University.

While hard work has long been a part of our culture, the County and its citizens have grown to realize the importance of having fun. From the passive enjoyment of listening to local bands and enjoying a sumptuous meal with friends, to activities such as aerobics, bicycling, boating, dancing, hot air ballooning and skateboarding, there seems to be a pastime for everyone. It is through these leisure-time activities that we experience joy, add meaning to our lives, build a sense of community and celebrate life. Thus, having fun is yet another part of the Baltimore County legacy.

"It is a happy talent to know how to play."

Ralph Waldo Emerson

An unidentified group of young men, women and children, seated on the lawn of George Vinton Bowen's house in Towson, enjoyed cool watermelon slices under a shade tree in the 1890s. (Photograph courtesy of the Baltimore County Public Library)

Clara Brown and Dorothy Baldwin played a nineteenth century board game called Crokinole. Dorothy was the daughter of Summerfield Baldwin, owner of the cotton manufacturing industry in Warren. This sedate recreation took place at Summerfield Baldwin's estate, Hillside Farm, facing the Gunpowder River, circa 1899. (Photograph courtesy of the Trustees of the Bunker Hill Foundation)

In the era of Babe Ruth, Fritz Mizel was a professional baseball player from Catonsville who played for several teams, circa 1910. (Photograph courtesy of the Catonsville Room, Baltimore County Public Library)

This three lane bowling alley on Reisterstown Road and Sudbrook Lane in Pikesville was originally owned by the Cox family, circa 1910. After Prohibition, Frank Spalding acquired the property and in 1933 turned the establishment into a bar and then eventually a restaurant. Spalding's stayed in business until the end of the twentieth century. (Photograph courtesy of the Baltimore County Public Library)

Gwynn Oak Amusement Park, in Woodlawn, opened in the 1890s and provided some of the most advanced rides and attractions of its era. The park held ethnic festivals, each lasting one week during the summer. The Dixie Ballroom was also a major attraction, where some of the greatest big bands came on Saturday nights including Goodman, Dorsey and Miller. The park was the site of pickets and protests for its policy on segregation during the early 1960s. The park closed after the destruction of Hurricane Agnes but was the inspiration for "Titled Acres" in the original movie *Hairspray*. (Photograph courtesy of the Baltimore County Public Library)

Lawrence Seicke was the proud owner of this 1910 era motorcycle and he had plenty of space in which to ride throughout the southwestern area of Baltimore County. (Photograph courtesy of the Catonsville Room, Baltimore County Public Library)

The Towson High School Band provided concerts all over Baltimore in 1917, a tradition continued by the current band more than ninety years later. (Photograph courtesy of the Baltimore County Public Library)

On a hot summer day, Bay Shore Park was a popular recreational facility located on the Chesapeake Bay. In a rather daring pose for 1922, Emma Vogal was photographed on the beach of the park. (Photograph courtesy of Jacques Kelly)

The "Sea Swing" was one of the most popular attractions at Bay Shore Park. The park was a popular resort between 1906 and 1947. (Photograph courtesy of the Dundalk-Patapsco Neck Historical Society Museum)

Less than a month after Charles Lindberg's solo trans-Atlantic flight, a celebration and parade for the "Lone Eagle" was held at Logan Field on May 21, 1927. General Douglas MacArthur was among the dignitaries who greeted Lindberg and his wife. (Photograph courtesy of the Dundalk-Patapsco Neck Historical Society)

Emulating a model in a 1930s magazine, Laura Smith struck a pose on the bumper of an out of state automobile. (Photograph courtesy of Louis Diggs)

Before the "blackouts" of World War II, the lights of the Alpha Theater in Catonsville were an impressive site after dark in 1940. The theater provided decades of entertainment for adults and children alike. (Photograph courtesy of the Historical Society of Baltimore County)

The 2nd Army Band performed at the Strand Theater on Shipway Road in Dundalk in 1952. The theater provided entertainment for the community from 1927, with the beginning of "talking pictures" until it closed in 1985. (Photograph courtesy of the Baltimore County Public Library)

From its opening in 1956, Hutzler's Westview store, with its distinctive concrete canopy entrance, was always festively decorated for Christmas and could be seen from the Beltway and Route 40. (Photograph courtesy of the Baltimore County Public Library)

Happy children sled down a hill on Pembroke Avenue near Flannery Lane in Woodlawn. No doubt, the children enjoyed an unexpected snow day in March of 1960. (Photograph courtesy of Jacques Kelly)

The Turner Station Basketball Team stopped practice long enough to have their picture taken. The team was part of the Turners Station Recreation Council which provided organized sports activities for children in the area, circa the 1960s. (Photograph courtesy of Baltimore County Public Library)

Cigarette boats raced at full throttle for the Governor's Cup at Cox's Point on Back River in Essex. The event was a Labor Day tradition in the 1960s. (Photograph courtesy of the Baltimore County Public Library)

Michael Crosby enjoyed the simple pleasure of jumping rope in the early 1980s. (Photograph courtesy of Baltimore County Public Library)

In 1987, during the 4th of July Parade, Drum Major Donald Fairhurst led his Washington Scottish Pipe and Band past Paul's Restaurant and the Hollywood Theater on Oregon Avenue in Arbutus. (Photograph courtesy of the Baltimore County Public Library)

The Valley View Tea Room, during the late 1980s, in the Towson Hutzler's Department Store, was a place where good friends, food and conversation could be celebrated. *Note the mural of Hampton Mansion on the wall and the little fox watching the hounds go by. (Photograph courtesy of the Baltimore County Public Library)

When she was playing professionally, Pam Shriver thrilled fans with her aggressive tennis style. Throughout her career, she won a total of twenty-two Grand Slam doubles titles and captured a women's doubles Gold Medal at the 1988 Olympic Games. Shriver continues to sponsor and support many sports related charities in the Baltimore area. (Photograph courtesy of the Baltimore County Public Library)

On August 26, 1989, hot air balloons lifted off from the Maryland State Fair Grounds and ascended in a colorful display over the Timonium and Towson skyline. (Photograph courtesy of the Baltimore County Public Library)

An unidentified young man soared down Oregon Ridge on his hang-glider in 1989. Spectators lined the side of the old ski slope to watch the dare-devil in action. (Photograph courtesy of the Baltimore County Public Library)

In 2004, to keep up with the interest in skateboarding, the Skate Bowl at Sandy Hills Park in Lansdowne was equipped with skateboard and rollerblade apparatus such as jumps, ramps, half-pipes and grinding rails. (Photograph courtesy of the Baltimore County Office of Communications)

An innovative science education show and concert, designed to spark students' interest in science was held at Deep Creek Middle School on September 25, 2006. The program, "FMA Live!" featured a Velcro wall, rocket launches and a hover chair among other technological attractions. NASA and Honeywell sponsored the program and demonstrated that learning can be fun. (Photograph courtesy of the Baltimore County Office of Communications)

Barney Wilson, formerly the Dean at CCBC Dundalk, and Bill Barry, Director of Labor Studies on the CCBC Dundalk campus, served as Masters of Ceremonies for the Dundalk Heritage Parade in 2007. In 2009, the parade, held every year on the 4th of July, will celebrate its seventy-fifth anniversary. (Photograph courtesy of Joe Giordano, *Dundalk Eagle*)

Regina Belle and Pieces of a Dream headlined the entertainment at the 11th Annual African American Cultural festival in the fall of 2007. The Spindels, Voices with Reason and the Calvary Crusaders were but a few of the additional groups who performed at this community celebration. (Photograph courtesy of the Baltimore County Office of Communications)

Sometimes just using your creativity is the best form of self-expression. No doubt these unidentified festival participants attracted a reasonable amount of attention in 2008. (Photograph courtesy of the Baltimore County Office of Communications)

This community activity proved that you could have fun as a "Cycle Santa" while raising money for holiday charities. (Photograph courtesy of the Baltimore County Office of Communications)

In recent years, Oregon Ridge Park has become the place to be on the 4th of July. With the Baltimore Symphony and choreographed fireworks, a picnic under the stars puts everyone in a patriotic mood. (Photograph courtesy of the Baltimore County Office of Communications)

Fans eagerly waited to cheer the Towson Tigers at the Unitas Stadium. Named for legendary quarterback, Johnny Unitas, the stadium serves as a tribute to his memory as the "golden arm" and one of Baltimore County's great athletes. Towson University has been important to the entire Unitas family with three of their children listed as alumni. Johnny Unitas, himself, even served at the University as the community ambassador for Towson athletes. (Photograph courtesy of Towson University)

Combining crabs, corn and a view of the water is one of the most enjoyable ways in which to spend a quite weekend in Baltimore County. With friendly service, Traci Sullivan has made the experience at Riverwatch Restaurant, previously the Seagull Inn for thirty years, even more enjoyable for her patrons. (Photograph courtesy of the Baltimore County Office of Communications)

Baltimore County Memories . . .

"I started going to the Strand Theatre in the heart of old Dundalk in the 1930s when movies were in the golden age but I didn't know it was the golden age. I only knew that I loved almost every film Hollywood sent my way."

- **Ben Herman,** *Red Trolley Days*

"Two old quarry holes, just south of St. Joseph's on Church Lane in the former town of Texas, were favorite swimming holes in the 1930s and 40s."

- **Claude "Greg" Gregory, Timonium**

"It was an especially cold winter in 1935 or 36 and Seneca Creek froze so thick that Norman Rice of Michigan, who was working at Glenn L. Martin Company, drove his Austin Healey on the Seneca and kept on going all the way out to the Chesapeake Bay."

- **Roay Ann McNamara, Seneca Creek / Middle River**

"In the mid 1940s, my brothers and I enjoyed the Snake Hole, later called the Dundalk Bathing Beach, where we learned to swim with instructors provided by the Red Cross. There was a large barge forty feet out into the water that gave us a place to which we could swim once we passed the beginner and intermediate lessons. The biggest reward and thrill was climbing up onto the barge to jump into the murky waters of the 'good ole Snake Hole'."

- **Naomi Kyte Binko, Dundalk**

"My favorite childhood memory is visiting the wonderful Bay Shore Park…A magical place on the Chesapeake Bay that is gone now but the memories will always be with me."

- **Donna Kuhar, Dundalk**

"Concerning Unitas Stadium at Towson University--It's nice to see something in Baltimore with Johnny's name… It's important for the whole community to remember him. He really was Baltimore."

- **Rick Volk, Former Colts Player and Friend**

"The athletic beltway rivalries were intense: Randallstown, Wilson Point, Woodlawn, Yale Heights, Lansdowne, and Baltimore Highlands."

- **Robert L. Ehrlich Jr., Governor of Maryland, 2002-2006**

"Back in the 1950s there was a drive-in named Willard's on Harford Road, just below Carney. The beltway now runs through where the drive-in was. Just about every teenager hung out there. Putty Hill Avenue was about a quarter mile south of Willard's and was on a hill. We all had old autos, and we raced up and down the hill with our hot rods. Then we would ride around Willard's showing our cars off. Those were the days. We would ride up and down Harford Road trying to pick up girls. We never got into any trouble with the law; it seems they knew we would not cause problems."

- **Rocco Rotondo, Parkville, Carney and Cub Hill**

"Growing up in the 1950s in Baltimore County was fun. Playing in the alley with kids of all ages…wearing a key to my skates around my neck while roller skating, playing jacks, making yards of chewing-gum wrappers…and going to the 5-and-10 to buy waxed lips and waxed bottles."

- **Lynn Skiar, Towson/Parkville**

"I enjoyed getting homemade ice cream and frozen custard from Curt's Drive-in on Belair Road in Fullerton."

- Ray Reider, Fullerton

"I remember riding the buses through Baltimore...we would go to the corner, get a bus to the waterfront and buy pigeons. Jim and I raised pigeons. My Dad would take Jim and I and some pigeons for a car ride. We would get out, let the pigeons go and when we got back home the pigeons would already be there."

Jack Wharton, Mount Washington

"I love Baltimore because it is so lively and exciting…I also like the fact that Baltimore County is very beautiful because it has wonderful natural resources like the Chesapeake Bay, forests and valleys."

- Stephanie Rountree, Age 10, Lutherville

"Most of all, I remember Report Card Day at Gwynn Oak Park. You would get in free if you showed a passing report card."

- David Gaine, Gwynn Oak

"No snow, no problem – we couldn't wait till the sawdust was delivered [on our farm]. It was stored in the barn, and a mountain of sawdust was just another adventure for us. We would climb up the hayloft with a flattened cardboard box and jump off and sled to the bottom of the sawdust pile…The rule was we had to be home by supper."

- Donna Ensor Reihl, Parkville

"When I was a small child in the early 1970s, my father would take me to Gwynn Oak Park in the summer. Dad would let me stand on his foot so that I met the height requirements to ride the Big Dipper roller coaster."

- Karen Ogle, Department of Environmental Protection and Resources Management Baltimore County Government

"I remember going to Druid Ridge Cemetery to visit Black Aggie on Halloween…It was pretty scary."

- Candace L. Croswell, Baltimore County Environmental Protection and Resource Management Baltimore County Government

"One of my favorite activities is the Lutherville-Timonium Recreation Council. They offer many different sports."

- Tarik Inman, Age 10, Lutherville

"I enjoyed growing up in the Cockeysville area. My family were members of Beaver Dam Swimming Club. It was located on Beaver Dam Road and had five different pools. The large pool was a quarry and had a swing and a high-diving board."

- Carol Brown, Cockeysville

"I am pleased that the African American Cultural Festival has become an annual fall tradition in Baltimore County… Thanks to the hard work from the members of the Festival, this event has become a great family event for all ages."

- Adrienne Jones, Founder of the African American Cultural Festival

"Through the 1960s, 1970s, 1980s and the 1990s, right through the new millennium, the Maryland State Fair has persevered … from the thrill of the midway to the grandeur of Thoroughbred racing and everything in between, the fair is truly 'the Eleven Best Days of Summer.'"

- Paige Horine, Timonium

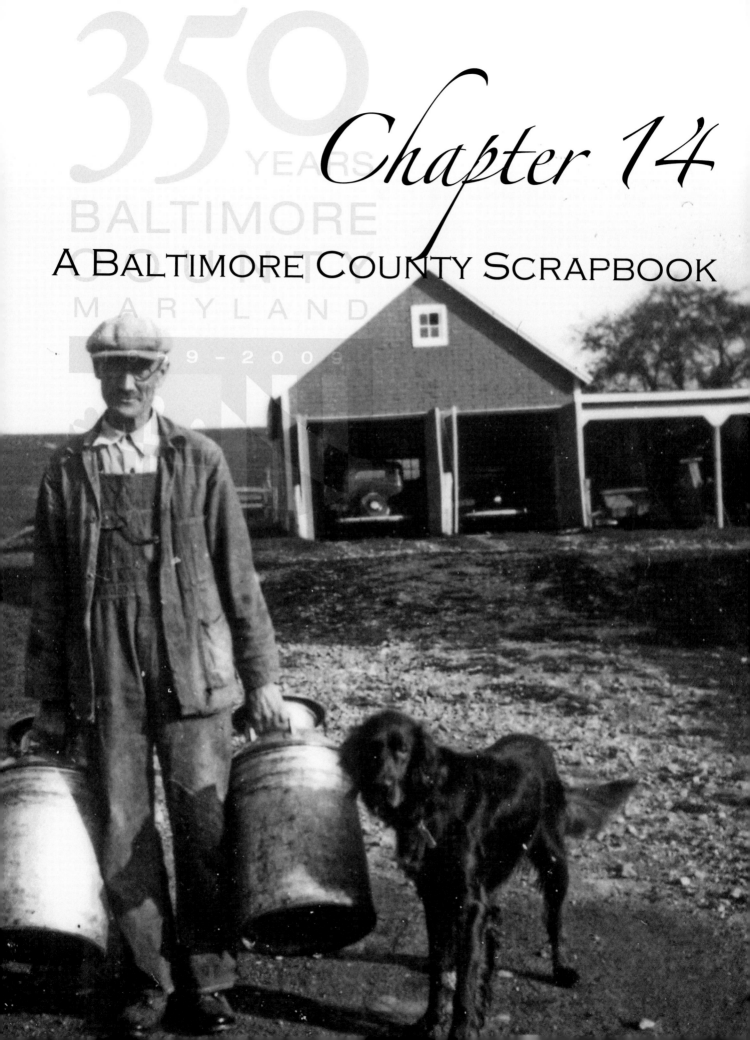

350
YEARS
BALTIMORE
COUNTY
MARYLAND
9 - 2 0 0 9

Chapter 14

A BALTIMORE COUNTY SCRAPBOOK

*O*ne of the most treasured heirlooms, collected over a lifetime is a scrapbook filled with the images of a family's existence. Like an album with faded pages of cherished loved ones, and those we can no longer identify by name but revere as ancestors, *A Baltimore County Scrapbook* endeavors to preserve the memories of the Baltimore County Family.

The photographs contained within this scrapbook reflect the serious along with the humorous side of life. They speak to the political, social and economic roles people have assumed within the community and they address the aesthetic and philosophical elements of our individual and collective human existence.

In most cases, the photographs were not taken by professional photographers, instead they were "snapped" by the average person who captured life as it was lived. In some cases, the photographs were staged while others were candid. Both, however, provide a sense of who we were, where we came from and how we developed into who we are today as a result of this heritage.

While the images are of specific people, places and events, occurring at a definitive time, they are representative of life experiences to which we can all relate. It is this shared heritage that creates a community and makes life in Baltimore County a rich experience full of personal memories. In many cases, these photographs transcend generations and speak for themselves.

While we prize the family scrapbook, the images not only reside within the pages of an album; they are indelibly etched in our minds. So too, are the images that represent Baltimore County. Thus, we leave behind *A Baltimore County Scrapbook* for the next generation.

"We are made wise not by the recollection of our past, but by the responsibility for our future."
George Bernard Shaw

John Charles Erdman proudly displayed his Grand Army of the Republic (GAR) medal. Private Erdman served as a Civil War cannonball maker from 1862-1865. It is believed that the commemorative medal was presented at a fiftieth anniversary ceremony, circa 1915. (Photograph courtesy of the Erdman Family)

Afternoon tea was served at Hillside Farm in Warren during the summer of 1893. Seated at the wicker table are Juliet Sewell Baldwin, Anne Louise Baldwin and Catherine Baldwin. Alice Woodward Leakin stood to the right. (Photograph courtesy of the Baltimore County Public Library)

George Upton, though pictured here without his trusty steed, was the first mounted policeman to patrol the Oella and Catonsville areas of Baltimore County in the closing years of the nineteenth century. (Photograph courtesy of the Catonsville Room, Baltimore County Public Library)

Will Owens and his lady were dressed in patriotic outfits on the 4th of July, 1905. While the "surrey with the fringe on top" brings to mind the musical *Oklahoma*, the photograph was actually taken in Reisterstown. (Photograph courtesy of J. P. Fitze and John McGrain)

Pierce Martin posed in 1909 with an unidentified lady wearing a most unique hat. (Photograph courtesy of J. P. Fitze and John McGrain)

This group of five young men should have known better than to attempt to make their own roller coaster. Needless to say, the experience ended in disaster during the first decade of the twentieth century. (Photograph courtesy of the Louise B. Goodwin Research Room, Reisterstown Branch, Baltimore County Public Library)

Daisy Stine and Herb Walters were the owners of Gwynn Oak Park, circa 1910. (Photograph courtesy of the Baltimore County Public Library)

Celebrating July 4th, 1911, the Reckord and Blackeney families pose in festive outfits. Raymond Reckord was at the wheel of a Model T Ford. He was the son of Walter P. Reckord, the first automobile dealer in Baltimore County. The Reckord's Ford dealership was operated out of his grist mill and supply warehouse on York Road in Cockeysville. (Photograph courtesy of the Margaret E. Haile)

The April 24, 1918 wedding of Elizabeth C. Kahl and Joseph B. Butts was taken at the St. Joseph Church in Fullerton. Joseph wore his World War I uniform. (Photograph courtesy of the Kahl Family)

Dewey Lowman was born in the Arbutus area in 1898 and enlisted in the Navy in 1917. He perished on the U.S.S. Cyclops with 310 of his shipmates. The American Legion Post and Unit in Arbutus were named in his honor. (Photograph courtesy of the Dewey Lowman Post #109, VFW)

A daring pose for 1920, Emily Stiffler (right) and friends showed off their ankles in the Stiffler Family yard. By the end of the decade, the "flapper" would make this scene commonplace. (Photograph courtesy of the Stiffler Family)

Standing on Sunset Hill in Parkton, an unknown girl was photographed by Emily Stiffler in 1920. The Parkton Methodist Episcopal Church could be seen at the left while the Calder Farm, at the corner of York Road and Stablersville Road, was visible on the right. (Photograph courtesy of the Stiffler Family)

Ruth Ruhl's wedding portrait typified the changing styles of the 1920s. She married Carroll Saumanin of Reisterstown. (Photograph courtesy of the Louise B. Goodwin Research Room, Reisterstown Branch, Baltimore County Public Library)

An undated aerial photograph showed the home of John and Cecelia Tanner at the intersection of Belair and Chapel Roads. A 7-11 store currently occupies the site. (Photograph courtesy of the Tanner Family)

Before the Depression, Sam Reed, who worked on the Charles Lord property near Shawan Road, carried milk pails to the road with his bird dog at his side. (Photograph courtesy of the Historical Society of Baltimore County)

Kenneth Spicer displayed the treats he received in his Easter basket, 1932. During the Depression, candy was an expensive treat. (Photograph courtesy of Emily Stiffler)

A Depression era graduation at Mount de Sales Academy in Catonsville was a joyous occasion. (Photograph courtesy of Baltimore County Public Library)

John Eli Diggs was born on March 14, 1846 as a free man, although his grandfather had been a slave in the town of Boring. While he was of modest means, this photograph of Diggs, during the Depression, portrayed him in a more affluent light. (Photograph courtesy of Louis Diggs)

F. Scott Fitzgerald and his wife Zelda surveyed the items which were salvaged after a 1934 fire at their Towson home called La Paix. At the time, Zelda was a patient at Sheppard-Pratt Hospital. (Photograph courtesy of Jacques Kelly)

The Oblate Sisters of Providence (OSP) were founded in Baltimore City in 1829. They bought the forty-seven acre Manning Estate in the Arbutus-Relay area in 1934. The property was used as a retreat house and novitiate until it burned in 1945. Four OSP novices stood in front of the main house with their new friend Frosty in 1939. (Photograph courtesy of the Oblate Sisters of Providence)

Mrs. Loraine Stephens pumped water at the town pump in Franklinville in November, 1942. (Photograph courtesy of Baltimore County Public Library)

In 1953, the Howard Price family posed for a portrait at Stockton Farms. With the children's outfits, the blended family is reminiscent of the Von Trappe Family. (Photograph courtesy of the Price Family)

The American Dream was embodied in this post World War II photograph. The new Dodge and modern suburban house on Oregon Avenue in Halethorpe belonged to George and Mabel Kirby. (Photograph courtesy of the Lanman family)

In the 1950s, porch swings were a favorite form of relaxation on warm summer nights. (Photograph courtesy of the Lanman family)

After a new fallen snow, circa 1955, Linden Avenue in Halethorpe was the picture of serenity. (Photograph courtesy of Edwin Hastry)

The typical kitchen in the 1950s looked quite basic when compared to its contemporary counterparts. The photograph was taken inside 4503 Maple Avenue in Halethorpe. (Photograph courtesy of the Lanman Family)

Dowell's Pond had been used for decades as a source of winter recreation for local residents. This ice hockey game occurred during the 1950s. Once a quarry, the pond was dangerous even with supervision and was drained and filled in after several drownings. The new Halethorpe Elementary School and the House of Good Shepard were built on the site known earlier as Dowell's Woods. (Photograph courtesy of Edwin Hastry)

After a big snow, the thrill of speeding down snow-covered streets kept children busy on their days off from school in the early 1960s. (Photograph courtesy of Edwin Hastry)

A quiet winter day on Ring's Farm was photographed circa 1960. Currently, it is the site of the Colony Apartments & Townhouses located between Arbutus and Halethorpe. (Photograph courtesy of Edwin Hastry)

The Baltimore County Public Library's Towson Bookmobile made a stop outside the churchyard wall of St. James in Monkton. Two children found a unique mode of transportation to the Bookmobile in 1960. (Photograph courtesy of Baltimore County Public Library)

Fredric Quentin Diggs rode one of his grandfather's horses in the early 1970s. The horses were used to plow William Washington's large garden on Winters Lane. (Photograph courtesy of Louis Diggs)

Glyndon celebrated its centennial in September, 1971. This young couple seemed to enjoy the festivities. (Photograph courtesy of the Louise B. Goodwin Research Room, Reisterstown Branch, Baltimore County Public Library)

A highly controversial sculpture "Winged Earth" was either loved or hated by the students and faculty of UMBC. This group of 1970s students gave their impression of the piece of art. (Photograph courtesy of Special Collections, Albin O. Kuhn Library & Gallery, University of Maryland, Baltimore County)

Three young students from Hebbville Elementary School, Steve Chapman, Niki Nalasnik and Kenny Semmont, prepared for a performance dressed as "California Raisins" in the 1988 Special Arts Day program held in Towson. (Photograph courtesy of the Louise B. Goodwin Research Room, Reisterstown Branch, Baltimore County Public Library)

Malvilyn Simpson Statham and Calvin Statham have given over forty-four years of community service in the southeast section of Baltimore County. Malvilyn sang with the Claraward Singers, sang backup for Elvis Presley and received the Stellar Gospel Award. Calvin has played piano for a variety of professional endeavors including music for the Walt Disney Company. (Photograph courtesy of Malvilyn and Calvin Statham)

James Karantonis went to school in Dundalk and after completing his graduate studies, went to work championing the cause of civil rights. His most significant achievement came when he was given the opportunity to work with Ms. Coretta Scott King planning the first national holiday honoring Dr. Martin Luther King, Jr. (Photograph courtesy of James Karantonis)

At a Waterfront Festival, an unidentified "Rosie the Riveter" posed with her daughter and demonstrated that the resolve that won World War II is still a part of the American spirit. (Photograph courtesy of the Baltimore County Office of Communications)

Adrienne A. Jones is the current Speaker Pro Tem of the Maryland House of Delegates, the first African American female to serve in that position in Maryland. Born in Cowdensville, an historic African American community located near Arbutus, Delegate Jones has served as the Director of the Office of Minority Affairs in Baltimore County (1989-95) and is the Executive Director of the Office of Fair Practices and Community Affairs in Baltimore County. (Photograph courtesy of the Baltimore County Office of Communications)

Emory Knode demonstrates a guitar at the Appalachian Bluegrass Shop on Frederick Road. With a family tradition in the music business since 1960, the sign says it all: "Everything for the Musician." (Photograph courtesy of the Baltimore County Office of Communications)

The Oriole seems to be everybody's favorite bird and it appeared that this police officer agreed. While real Baltimore Orioles have become increasingly rare in the region, Baltimore Oriole baseball spirit is alive and well. (Photograph courtesy of the Baltimore County Office of Communications)

On May 16, 2007, Radio Road in Pikesville was renamed Brooks Robinson Drive in honor of one of the greatest baseball players to ever take the field. The ceremony also included performances by the Pikesville High School Jazz Gospel Choir who sang Happy Birthday to the baseball legend on his seventieth birthday. (Photograph courtesy of the Baltimore County Office of Communications)

With a grand parade in Towson, Baltimore County celebrated Michael Phelps' return home after the 2008 Olympics. A graduate of Towson High School, Phelps won eight gold medals, more than any other athlete in Olympic history. (Photograph courtesy of the Baltimore County Office of Communications)

Citizens of Baltimore County came together at Fort Garrison to celebrate Thanksgiving in the tradition of the County's first settlers. (Photograph courtesy of the Oregon Ridge Nature Center)

The sharing of Native American culture has always been a popular part of festivals held at the Oregon Ridge Nature Center. The center also served as an archeological site supported by Baltimore County Public Schools. (Photograph courtesy of the Oregon Ridge Nature Center)

Young or old, attending a Baltimore County event on a warm summer day is an enjoyable experience. Sharing it with a best friend creates a memory that lasts a lifetime. (Photograph courtesy of the Baltimore County Office of Communications)

What could be more relaxing than sharing steamed crabs with good friends? While this contemporary scene is from Ship's Café in Catonsville, it represents a festive tradition repeated throughout the entire history of the County. (Photograph courtesy of the Baltimore County Office of Communications)

For three hundred and fifty years, simple pleasures of living in Baltimore County have been enjoyed by its residents. Passing on this way of life to the next generation will ensure the future of Baltimore County. (Photograph courtesy of the Baltimore County Office of Communications)

"Children are the living messages we send to a time we will not see."

Neil Postman

Map of Baltimore County - 2009

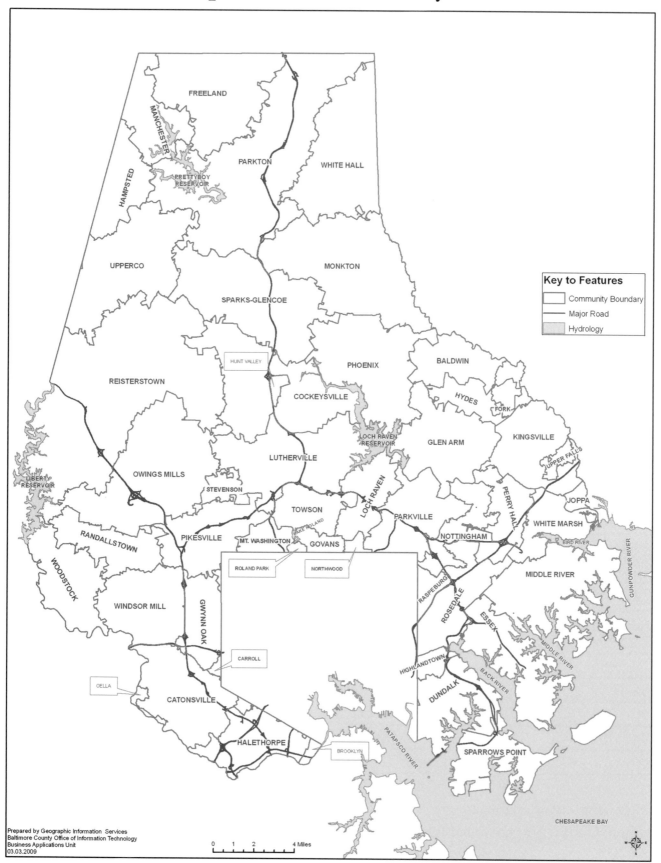

Key to Features
Community Boundary
Major Road
Hydrology

Prepared by Geographic Information Services
Baltimore County Office of Information Technology
Business Applications Unit
03.03.2009

0   1   2   4 Miles

Appendix B

The Legacy of Baltimore County's Population

1715	3,000
1756	18,000*
1771	28,000*
1800	25,434
1850	41,592**
1900	97,755**
1940	155,825
1960	492,134
2000	754,292
2004	763,181
2008	787,384 (estimated)

*   Includes the population of Baltimore Town
**   Reflects population loss due to the expanding size of Baltimore City

Appendix C

Baltimore County Executives

Service Years	Executive	Party
1956-1958	Michael J. Birmingham	D
1958-1962	Christian H. Kahl	D
1962-1966	Spiro T. Agnew	R
1966-1974	Dale Anderson	D
1974	Frederick L. Dewberry (Acting County Executive)	D
1974-1978	Theodore G. Venetoulis	D
1978-1986	Donald P. Hutchinson	D
1986-1990	Dennis F. Rasmussen	D
1990-1994	Roger B. Hayden	R
1994-2002	C. A. (Dutch) Ruppersberger III	D
2002-	James T. Smith	D

D=Democrat   R=Republican.
Baltimore County was governed by County Commissioners before 1956.

A Portrait of Baltimore County   2009

County Name

Baltimore was named for Cecilius (Cecil) Calvert, the second Lord Baltimore and the proprietor of Maryland, who in turn took his title from his barony estates in Longford County, Ireland.

County Seat

Towson is the largest unincorporated County Seat in the United States – 10,000 people live and work in Towson

General Statistics

Baltimore County is situated in the geographic center of Maryland, surrounding the City of Baltimore almost entirely. The County is the largest jurisdiction in the metropolitan area with a population in excess of 2.6 million. The City of Baltimore and Baltimore County are entirely separate political units.

Over the past few decades, the basic demography of the County has changed. Once predominately rural it is now an urban and rural mix. The County is the third largest land area of any political subdivision in the state of Maryland. Within its 612 square miles (plus an additional 28 square miles of water) are situated at least twenty-nine identifiable, unincorporated communities which, as of the year 2000, ranged in population from approximately 4,300 to 63,000. The County's overall population grew nine percent from 692,134 in 1990 to 754,292 in 2000. Today the County has the third highest population in the state of Maryland.

The total population of Baltimore County is larger than four states: North Dakota, Alaska, Vermont and Wyoming. Baltimore County is also more populated than the District of Columbia. (2000 U.S. Census)

Geography

Land area: 598.59 square miles
Persons per square mile as of 2000:   1,259

Population

Population by Race

Total Population, 2006	787,384	100.0%
One race	775,448	98.5%
White	541,197	68.7%
Black or African American	192,446	24.4%
American Indian and Alaska Native	2,324	3.0%
Asian	33,208	4.2%
Native Hawaiian and Other Pacific Islander	411	<0.1%
Other race	5,862	0.7%
Biracial or Multiracial	11,936	1.5%

Population by Sex

Total population 2006	787,384	100.0%
Male	374,023	47.5%
Female	413,361	52.5%

Population by Age

Total Population, 2006	787,384	100.0%
Under 5 years	46,559	5.9%
5 to 9 years	46,808	5.9%
10 to 14 years	50,328	6.4%
15 to 19 years	56,705	7.2%
20 to 24 years	52,258	6.6%
25 to 34 years	98,026	12.4%
35 to 44 years	116,354	14.8%
45 to 54 years	120,283	15.3%
55 to 59 years	48,385	6.1%
60 to 64 years	39,028	5.0%
65 to 74 years	52,891	6.7%
75 to 84 years	44,052	5.6%
85 years and over	15,707	2.0%
Median age (years)	38.8	

Source: US Census. American Community Survey 2006

Education and Work

Population by Education

Population over 25 years, 2006	534,726	100.0%
Did not complete High School	166,413	31.1%
High School Graduate (including equivalency)	149,588	28.0%
Associate Degree	35,372	6.6%
Bachelor Degree	105,762	19.8%
Professional Degree or Doctorate	77,591	14.5%

• *Newsweek* magazine's May 28, 2007 issue recognized nine Baltimore County high schools as being among the top 5% nationwide. Carver Center for Arts and Technology, Catonsville, Dulaney, Franklin, Hereford, Loch Raven, Parkville, Pikesville and Towson High Schools.

• Maryland School Assessment scores have risen consistently for the past four years.

• 140 of 163 BCPS schools made Adequate Yearly Progress according to the Maryland State Department of Education.

• In 2005-2006 10.7 percent of high school students took Advanced Placement (AP) exams. As the AP participation rate has climbed, BCPS has maintained a pass rate (now at 70.8 percent) higher than the national pass rate of 60 percent.

• The percentage of BCPS students taking the SAT (66.7 percent of the class of 2006) exceeds the national rate and has risen for five consecutive years.

• Private schools are an option for an alternate secondary education in Baltimore County, with 35,282 students attending various private schools. One hundred eighty eight private schools ranging from religious to alternative, provide a wide range of options.

Source: Maryland State Dept. of Education: Nonpublic School Enrollment, Community Survey 2006.

Population by Occupation

Employed civilian population 16 years and over, 2006	411,127	100.0%
Managerial, professional, and related occupations	171,168	41.6%
Service occupations	58,201	14.2%
Sales and office occupations	108,461	26.4%
Farming, fishing, and forestry occupations	444	0.1%
Construction, extraction, and maintenance occupations	33,206	8.1%
Production, transportation, and material moving occupations	39,647	9.6%

Population by Industry

Employed civilian population 16 years and over, 2006	411,127	100.0%
Agriculture, forestry, fishing and hunting, and mining	746	0.2%
Construction	27,040	6.6%
Manufacturing	29,604	7.2%
Wholesale trade	11,610	2.8%
Retail trade	43,534	10.6%
Transportation and warehousing, and utilities	19,991	4.9%
Information	9,551	2.3%
Finance, insurance, real estate, and rental and leasing	36,718	8.9%
Professional, scientific, management, administrative, and waste management services	51,354	12.5%
Educational, health and social services	101,191	24.6%
Arts, entertainment, recreation, accommodation and food services	29,884	7.3%
Other services (except public administration)	18,502	4.5%
Public administration	31,402	7.6%

Source: 2000 U.S. Census

Housing

Housing units, 2006	325,964
Homeownership rate, 2000	67.6%
Housing units in multi-unit structures, percent, 2000	27.7%
Median value of owner-occupied housing units, 2000	$127,300
Households, 2000	299,877
Persons per household, 2000	2.46
Median household income, 2004	$52,308
Per capita money income, 1999	$26,167
Persons below poverty, percent, 2004	8.2%

Business and Industry

Private non-farm establishments, 2005	20,657
Private non-farm employment, 2005	325,103
Private non-farm employment, percent change 2000-2005	3.4%
Non-employer establishments, 2005	55,261
Total number of firms, 2002	63,064
Black-owned firms, percent, 2002	12.4%
American Indian and Alaska Native owned firms, percent, 2002	0.7%
Asian-owned firms, percent, 2002	4.5%
Native Hawaiian and Other Pacific Islander owned firms, percent, 2002	<0.1%
Hispanic-owned firms, percent, 2002	1.5%
Women-owned firms, percent, 2002	27.0%
Manufacturers shipments, 2002 ($1000)	7,077,637
Wholesale trade sales, 2002 ($1000)	8,697,131
Retail sales, 2002 ($1000)	10,441,440
Retail sales per capita, 2002	$13,585
Accommodation and foodservices sales, 2002 ($1000)	1,110,178
Building permits, 2006	2,217
Federal spending, 2004 ($1000)	5,231,197

Mass Transit

Baltimore County residents use various forms of transportation to commute and travel. With ridership above 27,000 trips daily, the Baltimore Light Rail now runs 30 miles from the new Hunt Valley Town Centre in Baltimore County, through the heart of Baltimore City, past Oriole Park at Camden Yards, to BWI Airport. The Light Rail passes 32 stops from Hunt Valley. There is also service to Amtrak's Baltimore Penn Station. Through the extensive local highways system, people can easily live and work across the Baltimore Metropolitan Area.

Future Growth

Baltimore County, the largest municipality in the Metropolitan Area, increased its population 9.0 percent between 1990 and 2000. New population growth in Baltimore County is being directed toward the targeted growth areas—White Marsh to the east, and Owings Mills to the west. Designated as growth areas in 1979, each town center is adjacent to major transportation networks with regional shopping centers. White Marsh, which includes over 12,000 acres, has an estimated population of 78,000 people and is expected to grow to 92,000 by the year 2010. The Owings Mills community, which consists of 13,282 acres, has an estimated population of 65,000 people with the highest concentration of young, professional inhabitants in the County.

Statistics were provided courtesy of the Baltimore County Office of Communication.

Photographic and Research Acknowledgements

Groups and Organizations

Albin O. Kuhn Library & Gallery, University of Maryland, Baltimore County
Baltimore City, Division of Surveys and Records
Baltimore County Office of Communications, Bryan Dunn, Creative Director
Baltimore County Office of Economic Development, Fronda Cohen
Baltimore County Office of Planning and Zoning
Baltimore County Public Library
Barnard, Roberts and Co., Inc.
Beth El Congregation
Catonsville Room, Baltimore County Public Library, Lisa Vacari, volunteer
Community College of Baltimore County, Dundalk Campus, Bill Barry, Director of Labor   Studies
Dewey Lowman Post #109, Veterans of Foreign Wars
Dundalk Eagle
Dundalk-Patapsco Neck Historical Society
Enoch Pratt Free Library
James P. Gallagher and Greenberg Publishing Company, Inc.
Glenn L. Martin Maryland Aviation Museum
Goucher College
Granite Historical Society Nike Missile Base History Project Collection
Greater Parkville Community Council History Committee
Halethorpe Heritage Committee
Halethorpe-Relay Methodist Church
Hampton National Historic Site, National Park Service
Historical Society of Baltimore County
Legacy Web, Baltimore County Public Library
Louise B. Goodwin Research Room, Reisterstown Branch, Baltimore County Public Library
Maryland Historical Society
Oblate Sister of Providence
Oregon Ridge Nature Center
Relay Improvement Association
Special Collections, Albin O. Kuhn Library and Gallery, UMBC
The Sun
Towson University

Individuals and Families

The Birgel Family, Robert Bowen, The Christian Family, Jonathan M. Cornell, Louis Diggs, Paul E. Dimler, Jason Domasky, Dr. Andrew Dotterweich, Dr. Robert Y. Dubel, C. H. Echols, The Erdman Family, Middleton Evans, J. P. Fitze, Joe Giordano, Margaret E. Haile, Edwin Hastry, Mary Lou Hastry, Donald Hawkins, Jacques Kelly, Bill Hermann, William Hollifield, George Horvath, The Kahl Family, The Lanman Family, Dr. Barry A. Lanman, Jay Mallin, Dr. Anthony Marchione, John McGrain, Howard McNamara, Cliff Osborn, Richard Parsons, John Pinkerton, Dr. Mary Ellen Saterlie, The Stiffler Sisters, The Tanner Family, Elizabeth Klein Weimeister and Colonel Joe Zang

Bibliography

Anson, Melanie D. *Olmstead's Sudbrook: The Making of a Community.* Baltimore: Sudbrook Park, Inc., 1997.

Arbutus a Historical Scrapbook. Baltimore: Greater Arbutus Community Alliance, 2001.

Baird, Hulet C. *Edgemere.* Dundalk, MD: Dundalk-Patapsco Neck Historical Society, 1988.

Bartels, Fran. *Violetville, the History of a Neighborhood.* Baltimore: by the author, 2002.

Bonnett, Logie. *Baltimore County, its History, Progress and Opportunities.* Towson, MD: Jeffersonian Publishing Co., Inc., 1916.

Bready, Mary H. *Through All Our Days: A History of St. Paul's School for Girls.* Baltimore: Braun-Brumfield, 1999.

Brinkmann, Walter S. *Never-to-be-Forgotten Tales of Catonsville.* Baltimore: Press of Hoffman Brothers, Co., 1942.

Brooks, E. Nelson. *Growing Up in Arbutus in the 1930s and 1940s,* [s.l. : s.n], MD: by the author, 1995.

Brooks, Neal A. *A History of Baltimore County.* Towson, MD: Friends of the Towson Library, Inc., 1979.

Brooks, Neal A. and Richard Parsons. *Baltimore County Panorama.* Towson, MD: Baltimore County Public Library, 1988.

Bunting, Elaine. *Counties of Northern Maryland.* Centerville, MD: Tidewater Publishers, 2000.

Clemens, Shirley B. *From Marble Hill to Maryland Line: An Informal History of Northern Baltimore County.* Baltimore: Professional Printing Services, 1999.

Coale, Joseph M. *Middling Planters of Ruxton.* Baltimore: Maryland Historical Society, 1966.

County Directories of Maryland, Inc. *300th Anniversary Book of Baltimore County.* Baltimore: County Directories of Maryland, Inc., 1959.

Crewe, Amy Copper. *No Backward Step was Taken: Highlights in the History of the Public Elementary Schools of Baltimore County.* Towson, MD: Teachers Association of Baltimore County, Maryland, 1949.

Davidson, Isobel. *Real Stories From Baltimore County History.* Hatboro, PA: Tradition Press, 1967.

Diggs, Louis S. *From the Meadows to the Point: The Histories of the African American Community of Turner Station and What was the African American Community in Sparrows Point.* Owings Mills, MD: Uptown Press, 2003.

_____. *Holding On to Their Heritage.* Owings Mills, MD: Uptown Press, 1996.

_____. *It All Started on Winters Lane: A History of the Black Community in Catonsville, Maryland.* Owings Mills, MD: Uptown Press, 1995.

_____. *In Our Voices: A Folk History in Legacy.* Owings Mills, MD: Uptown Press, 1988.

_____. *North County: The History of African American Settlements in Northern Baltimore County's Scenic Horse Country.* Owings Mills, MD: Uptown Press, 2005.

_____. *Our Struggles: Historic African American Communities in Southeast Baltimore County.* Owings Mills, MD: Uptown Press, 2007.

_____. *Since the Beginning: African American Communities in Towson.* Owings Mills, MD: Uptown Press, 2000.

_____. *Surviving in America: Histories of 7 Black Communities in Baltimore County.* Owings Mills, MD: Uptown Press, 2002.

Dundalk the First Hundred Years 1895-1995. Baltimore: Patapsco Neck Historical Society, 1997.

Essex 1909-1999: 90 Years of Yesterdays. Essex, MD: Essex Revitalization and Community Corporation, Inc., 1999.

Forbes, Marie. *Speaking of Our Past: A Narrative History of Owings Mills, Maryland 1640-1988*. Bowie, MD: Heritage Books, 1988.

Fox, Jimmy. *Legacy of a Country Boy: Life on the Farm*. Falcon, CO: Fox Meadow Pub., 2007.

Frank, Beryl. *A Pictorial History of Pikesville, Maryland*. Towson, MD: Baltimore County Public Library, 1982.

_____. *Way Back When in Sudbrook Park*. Baltimore: Sudbrook Park, Inc., 1997.

Gontrum, Edwin K. *Sidelights on the History of Baltimore County*. Towson, MD: by the author, 1966.

Green Spring Valley, its History and Heritage. Vol. 1, A History; Historic Homes. Baltimore: Maryland Historical Society, 1978.

Green Spring Valley, its History and Heritage. Vol. 2, Genealogies. Baltimore: Maryland Historical Society, 1978.

Hahn, George H. and Carl Behm, III. *Towson: A Pictorial History of a Maryland Town*. Norfolk, VA: Donning Co., Publishers, 1978.

Hastings, Lynne Dakin. *Hampton National Historic Site*. Towson, MD: Historic Hampton, Inc., 1986.

Helton, Gary. *Dundalk*. Charleston, SC: Arcadia Press, 2005.

Herman, Ben. *Red Trolley Days*. Baltimore: Gameron Press, 2006.

Historic Long Green Valley, Baltimore County, Maryland: Architecture, History. Cockeysville, MD: Baltimore County Historical Society, 1981.

Hollifield, William. *Difficulties Made Easy: History of the Turnpikes of Baltimore City and County*. Cockeysville, MD: Baltimore County Historical Society, 1978.

Horne, Paige. *Maryland State Fair: Celebrating 125 Years*. Charleston, SC: Arcadia Press, 2006.

Huttenhauer, Helen G. and G. Alfred Helwig. *Baltimore County in the State and Nation*. Towson, MD: Board of Education of Baltimore County, 1962.

Jessop, Jennie E. *Origin Names in Baltimore County*. Cockeysville, MD: Publications Committee, Baltimore County Historical Society, 1967.

Kaufman, J.G. *Growing Up in Catonsville in the 1940s: A Home in Eden Terrace*. Catonsville, MD: [s.l. : s.n.] 2001.

Keidel, George C. *Early Catonsville and the Caton Family*. Baltimore: J.H. Furst Co., 1944.

_____. *Colonial History of Catonsville, Bicentennial Edition*. Catonsville, MD: American Bicentennial Committee of Catonsville, 1983.

Lanman, Barry Allen. *Halethorpe Heritage: Story of a Maryland Community*. Halethorpe, MD: Halethorpe Improvement Association, 2006.

Leifert, Donald L. *Riggie: Journey from 5th Street*. Parkville, MD: by the author, 2004.

Marks, David. *Crossroads: History of Perry Hall*. Baltimore: Gateway Press Inc., 1999.

Marks, Lillian Bayly. *Reister's Desire*. Baltimore: Garamond/Pridemark Press Inc., 1975.

Martinak, M. Linda and Angela Martinak Sutherland. *Essex and Middle River*. Charleston, SC: Arcadia Press, 2007.

McGrain, John W. *From Pig Iron to Cotton Duck, a History of Manufacturing Villages in Baltimore County*. Towson, MD: Baltimore County Public Library, 1985.

_____. *A Glossary of Place Names in Baltimore County, Maryland*. Towson, MD: Baltimore County Public Library, 1999.

_____. *Grist Mills in Baltimore County, Maryland.* Towson, MD: Baltimore County Public Library, 1980.

McKee, Ann Milkovich. *Hampton National Historic Site.* Charleston, SC: Arcadia Press, 2007.

Nickel, Jackie. *Essex.* San Francisco, CA: Arcadia Press, 2007.

_____. *"Old" Middle River: A Loving Look Back.* Easton, MD: Chesapeake Publishing Company, 2002.

O'Donovan, Molly. *Towson and the Villages of Ruxton and Lutherville.* Charleston, SC: Arcadia Press, 1999.

Orser, Edward and Joseph Arnold. *Catonsville 1880 to 1940 From Village to Suburb.* Norfolk, VA: Donning Co., 1989.

Perkins, I.B. *Picturesque Catonsville.* Baltimore: by the author, 1895.

Perry Hall: Reflections From the Past. Perry Hall, MD: Mercantile Bank & Trust, 1979.

Pollack, Carol. *Reisterstown, 1972.* Owings Mills, MD: Franz Printing Company, 1986.

Reflections, Sparrows Point, MD 1887-1975. Dundalk, MD: Dundalk-Patapsco Neck Historical Society, 1976.

Roberts, L. Keith. *History of the Back River Neck Peninsula.* Baltimore: Best Press, 1993.

Scharf, John Thomas. *History of Baltimore City and County.* 2 Vols. Philadelphia, PA: L.H. Everts, 1881.

Staab, Bob. *Growing Up in Dundalk: Precious Memories.* Baltimore: by the author, 2007.

Steffen, Charles G. *From Gentlemen to Townsmen: The Gentry of Baltimore County, Maryland 1660-1776.* Lexington, KY: University Press of Kentucky, 1993.

Toomey, Daniel Carro. *History of Relay, MD and the Thomas Viaduct.* Rev. 3rd ed. Baltimore: Toomey Press, 1995.

Villages of Northeast Baltimore County, Origins to c. 1940. Baltimore: Greater Northeast Baltimore County Historical District Committee, 1990.

Watson, Jerome R. *Churches of Turner Station: A Legacy of Faith and Family.* Turner Station, MD: Turner Station Heritage Foundation, 2002.

Wise, Marsha Wight. *Catonsville.* Charleston, SC: Arcadia Press, 2005.

Index

Dr. Barry A. Lanman is the Director of the Martha Ross Center for Oral History at the University of Maryland, Baltimore County. Concurrently, he is the past-director of the Consortium of Oral History Educators, historian for the Distinguished Flying Cross Society, an oral history consultant/interviewer and specialist in the field of oral history as an educational methodology. Dr. Lanman has authored numerous articles, pamphlets and books in the fields of education and history. He has also written and produced several educational and historical media presentations.

Barry A. Lanman received his doctorate from Temple University, served as the first chair of the Oral History Association's Committee on Education and is a founder and past-president of Oral History in the Mid-Atlantic Region. The Former Members of Congress named Dr. Lanman as its educator-historian for 1984 and he was recognized as a co-recipient of the Oral History Association's Postsecondary Teaching Award for 2008. Dr. Lanman has also received the Judith Ruchkin Research Award and the Forrest Pogue History Award.

Cover design by
Linda A. Schisler

Author photograph by
Linda A. Schisler

Published by the Historical Society of Baltimore County